GREATER MADISON

GREATER MADISON
Meeting the 21st Century

A Contemporary Portrait by Doug Moe

"Madison's Enterprises" by Jocelyn Riley

Produced in cooperation with the Greater Madison Chamber of Commerce

Windsor Publications, Inc.
Chatsworth, California

Windsor Publications, Inc.—Book Division
Managing Editor: Karen Story
Design Director: Alexander E. D'Anca
Photo Director: Susan L. Wells
Executive Editor: Pamela Schroeder

Staff for *Greater Madison: Meeting the 21st Century*
Senior Manuscript Editor: Jerry Mosher
Photo Editor: Larry Molmud
Development Editor: Amy Adelstein
Senior Editor, Corporate Profiles: Judith L. Hunter
Senior Production Editor, Corporate Profiles: Una FitzSimons
Customer Service Manager: Phyllis Feldman-Schroeder
Editorial Assistants: Kim Kievman, Michael Nugwynne, Michele Oakley, Kathy B. Peyser, Susan Schlanger, Theresa Solis
Publisher's Representative, Corporate Profiles: Sandee Frank
Layout Artist, Corporate Profiles: Chris Murray
Layout Artist, Editorial; Michael Burg
Designer: Alexander E. D'Anca

Library of Congress Cataloging-in-Publication Data
    Moe, Doug, 1956-
    Greater Madison : meeting the 21st century : a
    contemporary portrait / by Doug Moe.
    144p. 23x31 cm.
    Includes bibliographic references.
    ISBN 0-89781-313-8
    1. Madison (Wis.)—Description. 2. Madison
(Wis.)—History. 3. Madison (Wis.)—Industries.
4. Madison (Wis.)—Economic conditions. I. Title.
F589.M14M64   1990   89-24867
977.5'83043—dc20   CIP

Windsor Publications, Inc.
Elliot Martin, Chairman of the Board
James L. Fish III, Chief Operating Officer
Michele Sylvestro, Vice President/Sales-Marketing
Mac Buhler, Vice President/Sponsor Acquistions

This book is dedicated to Tony and Mary Anne Moe, who long ago decided Madison was better than a New York suburb as a place to raise a family.

And to Bette, who endured many late nights while this book was being written—some of which were spent working.

Frontispiece photo by Bruce Fritz

FACING PAGE: Some laid-back shutterbugs descend on the grounds at the state Capitol. Photo by Bruce Fritz

Contents

Introduction 9

Acknowledgments

I had a lot of help researching this book. I'd like to thank Bob Brennan and Bridget McCann-Horn from the Madison Chamber of Commerce; David Mollenhoff and Suzanne Voeltz from Downtown Madison, Inc. (David's excellent book on early Madison was particularly helpful in the history chapter); Lynn Russell at the Greater Madison Convention and Visitor's Bureau; Jack Gray, of the UW-Extension Recreation Resource Center; the unfailingly kind and helpful employees of the central branch of the Madison Public Library; Pam Schroeder, Amy Adelstein, Jerry Mosher, and the people at Windsor Publications; and, finally, Jim and Gail Selk and the staff of *Madison Magazine,* who not only provide a home base for an itinerent writer, but a fun home at that.

An old stone bridge at Tenney Park is the perfect place for a midday rest. Photo by Brent Nicastro

Introduction

It has been said Madison is not a single city, but several. It's easy to see why some people think so. Could there really be a place that provides big-city sophistication and small-town friendliness at the same time?

If there was such a city, it would be a place where on the same day you could see a Big Ten football game and hear a lecture from a Nobel Prize-winning professor . . . you could see a bill passed in the State Capitol and count the 200 varieties of lilacs in the 1,200-acre arboretum . . . you could sail on one of four lakes and peruse some of the world's finest art in nationally known museums . . . you could visit businesses engaged in work on the cutting edge of new technology, and you could buy gifts from craftsmen working outdoors on one of the country's most festive pedestrian malls.

You can do all of that, and much more, in Madison. The key to what makes Madison such an attractive place to live is the spirit of its people and the diversity of their endeavors. For instance, in 1987 *Inc.* magazine named Madison one of the 50 "most vibrant and fastest growing cities in the United States" in terms of job creation, corporate start-ups, and business growth.

While that would be a nice distinction for any city, it's even better—and more remarkable—when you consider that the very next year the group Zero Population Growth ranked Madison second (out of 192 cities nationally) in a "quality of life" study, the criteria of which included crime, education, water and air quality, and crowding.

Over the years Madison has been able to blend a commitment to economic development and the entrepreneurial spirit with an appreciation of culture, the arts, and sports, mixing in a fun-loving desire to enjoy life to its fullest. The result is a city that works hard, plays hard, and is many things but never dull.

The spirit often manifests itself in a commitment to excellence. A 1983 article in *Change* magazine assessing the results of seven major studies of academic excellence conducted since 1925 ranked the University of Wisconsin-Madison (UW-Madison) fourth-best in the United States.

Individual Madisonians also excel. Three UW-Madison professors have won Nobel Prizes while on the faculty. Madison native Eric Heiden won an unprecedented five gold medals for speed skating at the 1980 Olympics, while another city product, Andy

University of Wisconsin Band Director Michael Leckrone leads the way. Photo by Brent Nicastro

North, twice captured the United States Open, one of the world's most prestigious golf tournaments.

The city's business climate, as one might guess from the *Inc.* magazine honor, is vibrant. Unemployment through August 1988 was at a microscopic 2.2 percent. In the late 1980s, nearly all of the city's largest private employers—from meat packers to insurance companies to battery manufacturers—announced major expansions.

What may please Madisonians most as they prepare to meet the twenty-first century is the way the University of Wisconsin, city and state government, and private industry have adopted an attitude of cooperation, to the benefit of all.

Government, academia, and business—three diverse groups. But leaders from all three recently participated in a Dane County economic summit, which plotted a cogent course for the city and county's growth into the next century.

Perhaps what this demonstrates is that diversity is anything but a weakness—it's a strength. It has proven so in Madison—big city and small town—where economic growth and an excellent quality of life go hand in hand. It's true for Madisonians who live on a farm or in a lakefront condo, who attend symphonies or minor league baseball games.

With all its diversity, Madison is, after all, a single city—and a great one.

PART ONE

Madison Meeting the Challenge

The UW Band gets down at a football game at Camp Randall Stadium. Photo by Bruce Fritz

CHAPTER ONE

Historic Madison

I n 1948, when *Life* magazine called Madison America's most beautiful city, a salute to the glaciers of North America's Ice Age might have been in order. For it was the glaciers—or, more precisely, their retreat—which helped sculpt the area that would one day become Wisconsin's capital city.

The dumping of glacial debris and subsequent damming of glacial rivers formed four lakes, and, surrounding them, a series of gently rolling hills. Early settlers, encountering this natural splendor for the first time more than 10,000 years later, found their breath taken away. "I think," wrote author and militiaman J.A. Wakefield of the lakes in 1834, "they are the most beautiful bodies of water I have ever seen."

Today those lakes are straddled by a modern city bustling with life, a city of hardworking, fun-loving, spirited people, a city housing a great university, a state capital, and a diverse and vital business community.

How curious, then, to consider what else author J.A. Wakefield wrote back in 1834. Awed by the wilderness of the area now known as Madison, Wakefield observed, "It is not fit for any civilized nation of people to inhabit. It appears that the Almighty intended it for the children of the forest."

This early lithograph shows the emerging campus of the University of Wisconsin. Courtesy, State Historical Society of Wisconsin

If by "the children of the forest" Wakefield meant Indians, he was not as shortsighted as one might think. For close to 12,000 years, in fact, Indians had been the only human residents of the Dane County area.

Archaeologists believe small groups of Asians, now known as Paleo-Indians, slowly made their way to North America across land bridges that no longer exist. These people are thought to have arrived in the Madison area around 10,000 B.C.

Over the next 10,000 years, the Indians' way of life evolved in ways influenced by a general climatic warming. Along with hunting, they began growing and gathering their food. Hardwood forests replaced pines in the area.

A variety of tribes inhabited the land, but by the eighteenth century and the first coming of Europeans, the dominant tribe in what is now Madison was unquestionably

A Winnebago Indian woman is shown tanning a hide. Winnebagos were the dominant tribe in the area that is now Madison. Courtesy, State Historical Society of Wisconsin

the Winnebago. The Winnebago called the area "Taychopera"—region of the Four Lakes.

It is estimated that the white man first came to what is now Wisconsin in the late seventeenth century, when French-Canadian fur traders entered the area. Whether they made it as far south as the Madison area is open to question, although by 1768 a memoir by one Captain Carver titled "Travels through the interior parts of North America" made reference to the Blue Mounds, purportedly rich in lead and located in what is now western Dane County.

Five years earlier, in 1763, the French had signed over a large area of land, including Wisconsin, to the British in the Treaty of Paris. The land passed to American control following the War of 1812, though this fact had little effect on the grab bag of British and mostly French traders trapping beaver and muskrat in the area. The land was wilderness, individuals lived by their wits, so what difference did a piece of paper in a desk back East really make?

However, one document—a treaty between the Indians and the United States government signed in 1804—soon had a profound effect. In this treaty the Sauk and Fox tribes agreed to cede some 50 million acres of land, including much of what is now southern Wisconsin, to the United States, with the provision they could remain on the land until it was actually purchased by settlers.

By the mid-1820s the cultures were clashing, and in 1828 the U.S. government constructed Fort Winnebago at Portage. This led to the first white settling in Dane County and the first white man visiting the area that is now Madison: in 1828, traveling from his Blue Mounds cabin to Fort Winnebago, a lead prospector named Ebenezer Brigham camped at what is now Madison, and was so taken with the beauty of the area he predicted it would one day be a city—and a state capital. Brigham was clearly a prescient man.

Of course, all that still lay ahead. Meanwhile, relations between the Indians and the white settlers worsened, culminating in the last Indian war fought in Wisconsin, the Black Hawk War of 1832.

Black Hawk, the elderly chief of the Sauk and Fox tribes (he also had followers among the Winnebago), led his people in a bitter war that included fighting in the Madison area as the Indians were driven west. The war ended with the Battle of Bad Axe as 950 of Black Hawk's 1,000 braves were killed. Within weeks of that bloody battle, a treaty was signed that forced the Winnebago tribe out of the Madison area as of the following year, 1833.

Three years later, in 1836, the Four Lakes region, while not yet a town, would become capital of the territorial area. That remarkable transformation was largely the work of one energetic, personable, and extraordinary man—James Doty.

Doty. That a street in downtown Madison is named for him today hardly seems sufficient. For it was Doty, with perseverence and guile, who literally put Madison on the map. Such commitment was not, it should be noted, pure philanthropy on his part. Madison is a colorful city and James Doty was a colorful man.

Doty was a well-connected Detroit attorney in 1823, the year President James Monroe decided to appoint him circuit judge of the Western Michigan territory, which included the Wisconsin area. He spent the next nine years covering his expansive territory by canoe. Doty was tiring of this wilderness duty when in 1832 a new president, Andrew Jackson, appointed someone else to the judgeship, and our hero found himself back in private law practice.

This in no way set Doty back. Utilizing his knowledge of the untamed but soon to be settled Midwest, he became a land agent for several wealthy Easterners.

Land in and around Madison was first put on sale on August 1, 1835— the price was $1.25 an acre. When months passed and no one had purchased the isthmus area between the two largest of the Madison area lakes, Doty and a Michigan political friend bought 1,000 acres. Doty thought it had potential. Did it ever. The center of that tract of land is where Wisconsin's Capitol Dome now stands.

Doty would have to hustle if his land's potential were to be realized. The legislators of the Wisconsin territory—which was five times larger then than the current state of Wisconsin—were meeting in October 1836 in Belmont to choose a territorial capital, and ev-

The Battle of Bad Axe was a bloody defeat for Indians led by Black Hawk. After the battle, a treaty forcing Indians out of the area that is now Madison was signed. Courtesy, State Historical Society of Wisconsin

ery town with so much as crossing roads thought itself fit for the honor.

Doty didn't even have that much. Shortly before the legislative session began he had hired a Green Bay surveyor to lay out what Doty called "Madison City" —a grid of streets and lots centered on the isthmus. Appealing to the legislators' patriotic instincts, Doty named the streets of his paper city after the signers of the United States Constitution, and street names such as Bassett, Blount, Bedford, and Hamilton endure in Madison today. For the city itself, Doty chose the name of the recently deceased "Father of the Constitution," James Madison.

Incredibly, though no town existed and only one legislator had even seen the area (Ebenezer Brigham, who loved it), Doty carried the day. By one vote, on November 23, 1836, Madison was named the territorial capital. Bemused observers of the legislative process credited Doty's charm and salesmanship for the victory; others less charitable spoke of under-the-table payoffs to legislators, allegations which were never proven.

In any case, the first and most important seed of Madison's growth had been planted: it was the capital. And just as today much of the city's identity and commerce owes to its being a seat of government, so did the first business to open in Madison.

On the way home from the landmark Belmont session, a few legislators stopped at the Blue Mounds home of Eben Peck (a friend of Ebenezer Brigham) and informed him of the decision to make Madison the capital. Peck could have been forgiven for asking, "What is Madison?" (Remember, there were only five white people living in all of Dane County at this point). Instead he realized the new capital's potential for turning a profit, and with his wife Rosaline he

established, in the spring of 1837, the Peck Tavern—later the Madison House—a wood cabin complex designed to lodge, feed, and provide liquid refreshment for legislators when they weren't pondering the affairs of state.

It must be said that accommodations were not exactly plush in the Pecks' place or in any of the few other establishments set up to accommodate the legislators. In desperation some of the visiting lawmakers secured lodging in private homes, although this was difficult in that by 1844 there were only 216 residents in all of Madison.

Worse, the Capitol building itself wasn't finished (in its first incarnation) until 1844, and early legislative sessions were held in a local hotel. Then when the Capitol *was* completed, the roof leaked.

Not surprisingly, movements sprang up regularly to move the capital to a more suitable site—most of the anti-Madison people favored Milwaukee. They were thwarted by an intense public relations campaign by loyal Madisonians, a campaign which not insignificantly is said to have included free booze for fence-sitting legislators who agreed to fall into the Madison camp.

The truth is, Madison's first decade was distinguished more by uncertainty than by growth, although a move in 1846 from county to village government was a decided step toward self-determination. The next decade would be far more productive, culminating in Madison gaining a city charter by 1856.

Many other positive advances had occurred by that time, most notably in 1848, when Wisconsin officially became a state and Madison was named site of the state university. Statehood meant the end of the threat

to Madison's status as capital, and the university—well, the University of Wisconsin-Madison has meant so much to the city over the years that its impact is impossible to overestimate.

On June 12, 1838, an endowment of public lands for an institute of higher education was provided by the legislature, and while not much happened for nearly a decade, at that time regents were appointed, state government was inaugurated, and an act to take effect in 1848 was passed, specifically incorporating the university "at or near the seat of government." The formal inauguration of the first chancellor, John H. Lathrop, took place in January 1850. The first university buildings were soon erected, and in 1854 the first class, consisting of two people, graduated.

Madison was now more than a paper tiger. It had tangible assets to promote besides its great beauty: a permanent state capital, a university, and a growing business community.

What was needed now was someone to do the promoting, a galvanizing force, an energizing personality who could do for the new Madison what James Doty had done for the paper city. In late 1848 the void was filled when Leonard James Farwell moved to Madison.

Farwell was a Milwaukee businessman who had in fact become sold on Madison's potential a year earlier, when, at the age of 28, he purchased much of the land originally belonging to Doty.

Farwell soon became a one-man dynamo for Madison. He traveled to attract foreign immigrants, stressed the beauty of the region, got streets and canals built, and named the lakes from Indian lore (Mendota, which meant "great," for the largest, and Monona, which meant "beautiful," for the other lake bordering the isth-

mus). By 1850, three years after Farwell's initial interest in Madison, the village's population had doubled and 100 new buildings had been built, including, in 1849, a new courthouse.

Of course, all of Farwell's promoting would have gone for naught had not Madison been an appealing place to live and visit. Legendary newspaper editor Horace Greeley, in Madison for a lecture in March 1855, called it "the most magnificent site of any inland town I ever saw . . . The University crowns a beautiful eminence a mile west of the Capitol . . . Madison is growing very fast . . . She has a glorious career before her."

Farwell quickly hired Greeley to print 10,000 copies of his comments, along with a map.

Another lecturer, Bayard Taylor, wrote in a letter to the *New York Herald Tribune*: "For natural beauty of situation, Madison is superior to every other Western city that I have seen."

The early 1850s boom enjoyed by the city was widespread and included the arrival of the first railroad in 1852. New stores seemed to open almost daily, and between 1852 and 1856 seven banks opened their doors in Madison.

Prosperity brought leisure time, and local residents hunted, fished, drank beer (there had been a heavy German immigration), and sailed. They also skated upon Madison's lakes in the winter just as, more than a century later, a young boy named Eric Heiden would grow up preparing himself for a brilliant Olympic career.

As might have been expected, the unprecedented boom was followed by a downturn in the local economy, precipitated in part by an economic slide in the East. But like the rest of the country, Madisonians soon had other things to worry about besides their sluggish economy. The country was readying for war.

If the praise of such nationally known personalities as Horace Greeley hadn't gained Madison prominence throughout the country, the Civil War did. A large number—70,000—of the 91,000 men whom Wisconsin sent to the front were lodged and trained at Camp Randall in Madison. Purchased by the state in 1893, the property is now an athletic stadium for the university as well as a preserved historical site under the same name: Camp Randall.

The Chicago, Milwaukee & St. Paul Railroad and Depot at West Washington Avenue in Madison was a busy transportation hub. Courtesy, State Historical Society of Wisconsin

Madison's first militia had in fact been established in 1858. The truth is, Madisonians and Wisconsin citizens as a whole were not up in arms over slavery. A statewide referendum on black suffrage in 1857 was rejected by a ratio of 5-1 statewide and 3-1 in Madison.

But that didn't mean the city wasn't angered by the actions of Southern states, particularly in regard to secession. When South Carolina seceded in December 1860, Governor Alexander Randall told the Wisconsin legislature a month later, "Secession is revolution, revolution is war, and war against the government of the United States is treason." The day before the governor's speech, in fact, a Madison militia called the Madison Guards had volunteered their service to Randall in case it "might be required for the preservation of the American Union."

Before long, it was. In April, Fort Sumter, a South Carolina base occupied by Federal troops, fell to Confederate batteries. In the rush of Wisconsin units to join the fight, Madison led the way, prompting a Milwaukee newspaper to say Madison "takes the palm for patriotism."

But enthusiasm for the war, as often happens after the reality of bloodshed and lost lives replaces patriotic rhetoric, flagged in Madison. Residents were disturbed by the rowdy trainees at Camp Randall. By 1862 the city was having a problem meeting its quota of soldiers ordered by President Abraham Lincoln and a draft was narrowly averted, although some local authorities asserted Madison hadn't been credited for its outpouring of volunteers in the war's early stages. A year later, a draft was instituted.

In any final analysis, however, Madisonians more than did their part for the war effort. By the spring of 1865, it was estimated that two of every three Madison men aged 20 to 45 were fighting for the North. An official report at the war's end showed Madison with the largest number of soldiers per capita of any Wisconsin city. Madison's Civil War record is a proud one.

After the war, returning soldiers with back pay in their pockets helped boost the local economy. And fun returned to the city, as Madison got its first pipe organ (in the Grace Episcopal Church) in 1867, the same year

Camp Randall in Madison was a Civil War camp where many Wisconsin men fighting in the Civil War were housed and trained. Today the area is the site of the University of Wisconsin football stadium—Camp Randall. Courtesy, State Historical Society of Wisconsin

the first steamboat was launched on Lake Mendota.

Community leaders were anxious for the city to get back down to business. Some Madisonians were leary of what manufacturing would do to the aesthetics of the city, but businesspeople pointed out that natural beauty and a good university alone do not a city make. It was a growing partnership between these two factions—the commercial and the aesthetic—that formed a solid base for the Madison of today and, indeed, of tomorrow.

In the two decades following the Civil War, Madison slowly began to evolve not only as a service industry and commercial center based largely on tourism and the rapid growth of the University of Wisconsin; it also began to attract manufacturing.

One of the first companies to locate in Madison was Fuller and Johnson Manufacturing, incorporated in 1880 as a farm implement company. Its offshoot, the Gisholt Machine Company, a machine tool manufacturer, remained a major economic force in Madison for much of the next century. Maybe Madison could be an industrial city after all.

A factory district of sorts began to develop on the city's East Side. Some manufacturing concerns came and went, others endured. In 1902, for instance, Madison had nine cigar factories; by 1950 they had all disappeared.

Other manufacturers who first appeared in the early twentieth century are still going strong. The Oscar Mayer meat processing company established their first Madison plant in 1919, employing 400 people, and they remain the city's largest private employer.

The French Battery and Carbon Company, predecessor to Rayovac, moved to Madison in 1907. In 1986 Rayovac completed a multimillion-dollar new world headquarters in the city.

Madison's ability to retain its physical beauty and flavor as a university town (it has been called the "Athens of the Midwest"), while at the same time encouraging business, is a tribute to the cooperative spirit that forms the foundation of Madison today. For the story of twentieth-century Madison is one of an unparalleled melding of state government, the University of Wisconsin, a truly booming service industry (the city has become an internationally known medical and insurance center), the continuing presence of founding companies such as Oscar Mayer and Rayovac, and finally, the city's bright new business light: the high-technology industry for which the University of Wisconsin is an invaluable hub.

That spirit of cooperation will carry the city into the twenty-first century as well.

LEFT: This photo of Madison's central business district was taken by aerial kite near Lake Monona in 1908. In the background of the isthmus is Lake Mendota. Courtesy, State Historical Society of Wisconsin

BELOW: The French Battery and Carbon Company was the predecessor to Rayovac Battery Company. Rayovac still maintains its world headquarters in Madison. Courtesy, State Historical Society of Wisconsin

CHAPTER TWO

Downtown Renaissance

C ities relish symbols—a building, a monument, something instantly recognizable and identified with the city. Those that don't already have a striking showpiece along the lines of, say, the Golden Gate Bridge in San Francisco, are usually in the process of trying to create one.

Madison's centerpiece is among the nation's oldest and most impressive. The State Capitol, on the isthmus between Madison's two largest lakes, dominates the city's skyline with a shining dome of steel and granite. Majestic yet rich in colorful lore, it *is* Madison.

The Capitol forms the heart of downtown Madison, an area graced with a splendid physical setting, resting as it does on a 3,000- to 6,000-foot wide isthmus separating Lakes Mendota and Monona. On soft summer nights when residents and visitors alike gaze across the lakes to Madison's downtown, the splendor of the Capitol can leave them breathless.

Over the years, the city's downtown has developed a personality to match its physical splendor. The wings of the Capitol building, designed at right angles pointing to the four points of a compass, form a square, and it is the Capitol Square that informs much of

An ultralight takes off from Lake Monona, a body of water that proved quite profitable during Wisconsin's ice-harvesting years. Photo by Bruce Fritz

Designed at right angles, the wings of the Capitol building point to the four points of the compass. Photo by Bruce Fritz

the downtown's personality.

The Square is where Madisonians congregate, on and around the 13-acre Capitol Square Park. It's where you can hear free concerts, attend art fairs and farmer's markets, and eat at fine restaurants or on a picnic blanket after visiting one of dozens of street vendors.

It's a place to see and be seen. For people-watchers the feast is varied, unending, and egalitarian. On the Capitol Square you'll see the governor of the state putting a dollar into the guitar case of a street troubadour and the speaker of the state assembly taking five minutes to tell a group of tourists how to get to a historical museum.

The Capitol Square, then, is Madison's answer to Faneuil Hall in Boston. A walk around the Square is invigorating, the energy there almost palpable.

The Square is teeming with movers and shakers—but that's not all. The city's cultural pulse may be taken in the area as well. It's been estimated there are 6 million books within six blocks of the Capitol building. That includes a number of libraries and bookstores. Just six blocks from the Capitol (six blocks along State Street, which may be the most entertaining six blocks in America), the University of Wisconsin campus begins. Madison's Civic Center (the sight of major national touring productions) and Art Center are even closer—you can see them from the Capitol steps. And not only is the Capitol itself the seat of state government, Madison's city hall and courthouse are just a half-block away.

At a time when downtowns across the country are struggling to find identities, Madison's has found an enviable one. Downtown is where the action is. It has been an evolutionary process, of course. While the Capitol has always been on the Square, other dynamics of the area have changed over the years.

For much of this century, the Capitol Square was a retail center. But as Madison grew in the years after World War II, the growth was mainly west and in conjunction with the ever-expanding University of Wisconsin. Large, attractive shopping malls began to appear and some retailers, the large department stores in particular, headed west to the malls.

There was, at first, a concern that the departure of large retailers would hurt the downtown significantly. Would people quit coming downtown, and as a consequence would life go out of the heart of the city?

Fortunately, many businesses and professional firms recognized an opportunity to be near the seats of state and local government, as well as the county courthouse. New office construction in the downtown in the 1970s and 1980s has been nothing short of amazing. Some of the structures—like the First Wisconsin Plaza and Manchester Place, each right on the Capitol Square—are architecturally stunning.

From 1978 to 1984 a total of 492,000 square feet of office space was either built or rehabilitated in the downtown area. Over the same period a total of $186 million was invested there.

Today, downtown is where you find the state's top law firms, lobbyists, political campaign headquarters, brokerage houses, consultants, and, of course, the majority of the state government agencies. There may not be a department store in sight, but it's probably the highest-powered business district in Wisconsin.

With all those office workers, it's not surprising that a number of new restaurants, theaters, and specialty shops also opened downtown. Then, too, people like living close to work; the last decade has brought a number of classy condominium developments and other housing to the downtown area.

It was an evolution all right, if not quite a revolution. What was needed was direction, and in the early 1980s an extraordinary partnership was formed to help

A seemingly submerged replica of a national symbol forms a striking vista in front of Memorial Union at the University of Wisconsin. Photo by Bruce Fritz

A Capitol tour is a
must for Madison visit-
ors and residents alike.
Photo by Bruce Fritz

provide just that.

Downtown Madison, Incorporated (DMI), a nonprofit, private-sector coalition of downtown businesspeople, has become the acknowledged leader of Madison's downtown renaissance. DMI's paid staff, with the help of tireless volunteers from downtown businesses and city government, first studied the area, then identified and promoted its assets and suggested courses of action. They've been rewarded with a thriving downtown that will move with Madison into the next century.

Most observers believe the downtown's success is due mainly to the effective utilization of the area's natural strengths. It only made sense to locate new office space near the State Capitol and city hall. Add the great views, the nearby lakes—why would someone want to work anywhere else?

For flavor and spice, DMI has helped to either create or promote a number of events that draw thousands of people downtown. Once they see the natural beauty, the restaurants, the wide variety of intriguing specialty shops, and the festival-like atmosphere of the Capitol Square, most people are hooked.

The special events span the entire calendar year. Beginning in late June and running until early August, the Wisconsin Chamber Orchestra, under the direction of David Crosby, performs on the steps of the State Capitol every Wednesday. This free, enormously popular series began in the early 1980s and is credited with bringing a lot of people to Madison's downtown for the first time. The crowds have been estimated at up to 20,000 people. Picnic lunches are sold by local restaurants, and people bring blankets and lay back while the beautiful music seems to celebrate the city in the gathering dusk. At one recent concert a Madison woman pointed dreamily at the Capitol dome and the lake beyond and said, "You know, when you live here it's easy to forget how beautiful it all is."

The festival-like atmosphere continues downtown all summer, manifesting itself in a variety of ways. Every Saturday morning, area farmers rise before dawn and cart their fresh fruit, vegetables, and breads to the Capitol Square for the Farmer's Market.

From 6 A.M. to 2 P.M. Madisonians face the kind of tough decision most city dwellers only dream of: How many pounds of wonderful fresh produce can they reasonably carry back to their cars? Friendships form at the Farmer's Market; both farmers and customers

have been coming for years. Many Madisonians have personal favorites and will suffer another farmer's sweet corn only if store-bought is the only alternative.

A smaller version of the weekend Farmer's Market is held in the summer on Wednesdays at noon just off the Square on Martin Luther King, Jr., Boulevard, the street running south from the Capitol to Lake Monona. The street was originally named Monona Avenue, and Madison's city-county government building is located there. In 1986 the street name was changed to honor the slain civil rights leader, a move much in keeping with Madison's progressive ideals.

The sports bug bites the downtown every spring. In May, before the start of the Farmer's Market, bicycle races are held around the Capitol Square. Eric Heiden, one of Madison's favorite sons and an Olympic speed skating legend, spent some time on the pro bike-racing circuit, and when he returned to Madison for a race one spring the crowds poured out in tribute.

The third Saturday in July brings the Paddle 'N Portage Canoe Race, not for the couch potato or anyone in less than tip-top shape. The race attracts over 600 canoeists from all over the Midwest. It begins at James Madison Park with participants canoeing across Lake Mendota, then portaging (carrying!) their canoes across the isthmus to Lake Monona, and finally canoeing across *that* lake to Law Park, where they collapse like beached whales.

This author believes the best way to participate in the race is from a window table in the bar of the Fess Hotel Restaurant. The Fess is located a block off the Capitol Square on east Doty Street. It's a historic building—the hotel was originally built in 1848. The upstairs now serves as office space while the main level is a popular bar and restaurant, from which one might wave at the Paddle 'N Portage canoeists as they race across the isthmus.

The Fess, like a number of downtown Madison eating and drinking establishments, has a garden for outdoor dining in nice weather. Just up the street the newly opened Cafe Europea provides sidewalk tables which really do invoke the flavor of a Parisian cafe.

One of the more popular events of the summer in Madison is the annual Art Fair on the Square, held the second weekend in July on the Capitol Square (there is also an art fair *off* the Square held at the end of Martin Luther King Boulevard opposite the Capitol). In recent years the Art Fair has been favorably compared to the

The Paddle 'N Portage Canoe Race is getting underway. Photo by Brent Nicastro

best summer art fairs nationally. Close to 500 artists from all over the United States and Canada turn the Square into a breathtaking outdoor gallery.

Just a couple of months later it becomes a taste-tempting restaurant when the Taste of Madison, a Labor Day weekend tradition since 1983, gets the Square cooking. More than 50,000 people annually come downtown to feast on fine food from city restaurants, hear live music, see live theater and comedy, and generally enjoy themselves as the city bids farewell to summer.

As many as 55 restaurants serve up limited portions (nothing costs over $2) of everything from barbecued ribs to fudge bottom pie. The challenge of the Taste of Madison, much easier said than done, is to eat a little of a lot.

Much of another ambitious, popular event is held in Madison's downtown in September. The Festival of the Lakes, a five-day spectacle of music, dance, stage, and visual imagery, debuted in Madison in 1986, was held again in 1988, and seems destined to become a benchmark of the downtown's growing mix of culture, fun, and excitement.

The folks at DMI have even managed to heat up the central city during everyone's favorite month in Madison—January. Beginning in 1986 the annual Winter Carnival has helped Madisonians and visitors forget their dripping noses and chattering teeth.

The three-day carnival includes snow and ice sculpting competitions, a snowball softball tournament, hay rides, an ice-fishing shanty painting contest, and, finally, the Frostiball—a dazzling gala held right in the State Capitol (the first year). Beneath the fabled Capitol dome, hundreds of formerly attired Madisonians sip complimentary champagne and dance to orchestra music.

The Capitol itself, of course, is one of downtown's—and the city's—top attractions. The Capitol building was renovated and enlarged a number of times during its first decades of existence. The construction of the fourth and present Capitol took about 10 years, beginning in October 1906 and ending in 1917, at a cost of more than $7 million. (A fire in 1904 had destroyed a large part of the building's interior.)

The Capitol's commanding feature, the dome, is by design just several inches shorter than the Capitol dome in Washington, D.C. Someone decided at the last minute that it would be inappropriate to have the Wisconsin dome taller than that of the nation's Capitol.

It is nevertheless impressive. Wisconsin's is believed to be the one granite dome in the United States and is supported by approximately 2,500 tons of steel.

Atop the dome stands a gilded bronze statue of a woman named "Wisconsin" and meant to symbolize the state motto, "Forward." Everyone refers to the statue as "Miss Forward." She is indeed worthy of respect: over 15 feet in height and weighing over 3 tons. On the crest of her helmet (at a height of 285 feet), is a badger, the state animal. In her left hand she holds a globe surmounted by an eagle.

The grounds and exterior of the Capitol are impressive, but it is the interior which truly inspires awe. One can see immense arches, marble columns, and the sure-fire crowd-pleaser: the unobstructed view of the interior of the great dome, 76 feet in diameter and highlighted by a ceiling painting by the distinguished artist Harry Blashfield. Even worldly politicians and dignitaries, casting a quick glance skyward, have been left gaping at the imagery. It's really something, and one reason a Capitol tour is a must for visitors and residents of Madison.

The Capitol is not the only historic building in the downtown area, of course. In 1988 the Madison Landmarks Commission published a booklet titled "Madison's Pioneer Buildings" to let everyone in on the city's interesting and varied past.

The historic buildings include the Grace Episcopal Church, 6 North Carroll Street, the only church still standing out of four that were on the Capitol Square in the nineteenth century; Keenan House, 28 East Gilman Street, built in 1857 in a German Romanesque Revival style; the Stoner House, 321 South Hamilton Street, a two-story Italianate building; and the Hooley Opera House, 120-128 East Pickney Street, which served as Madison's first theater.

The downtown street names provide an interesting and little-known piece of Madison lore. Do the ones listed above—Carroll, Gilman, Hamilton, and Pinckney—ring any bells? They should, at least for any student of United States history.

When James Doty laid out a design for Madison in 1836, during his attempt to have it selected state capital, he thought his "paper city" would look more real to legislators if the streets were named. Doty decided to name the streets after the signers of the United States Constitution, and the city itself after the man called the "Father of the Constitution," James Madison.

Greater Madison

A number of small cities and towns that border Madison contribute to the economic vitality of "Greater Madison." These communities occasionally struggle for an identity separate from the capital city, but the relations are generally good and the neighboring communities retain some hometown pride.

Middleton, located just west of Madison, has a population of over 13,000 and more than 400 businesses. By the late 1980s some observers were touting Middleton as the fastest developing economic area in Dane County.

Notice was served in 1988 when prominent national developer John Hammonds announced plans for a new, 10-story Holiday Inn hotel-convention center complex that would be located west of the Beltline Highway in Middleton.

Shortly after Hammonds' announcement, a Middleton developer, Jeff Straubel, unveiled plans for Greenway Center, on 220 acres of Middleton. The Greenway Center development would include Hammonds' Holiday Inn project along with additional office space and retail stores.

In late 1988, the M&I Bank of Madison announced they would be building a major new branch in Middleton near the Greenway Center property. The new building was projected to cost $4 million with six stores and 80,000 square feet of office space. It will be named after its signature tenant—the M&I Bank Tower.

Middleton may well lay claim to being the hottest financial center in the Greater Madison area. It has long been home to one of Dane County's hottest manufacturing companies, Tracor Northern.

Tracor Northern, which makes a wide array of machines used in medicine and industrial research, has an 85,000-square-foot plant located at 2551 West Beltline Highway in Middleton.

Tracor Northern designs and manufactures X-ray microanalysis, image processing, and optical spectroscopy systems and also makes monitoring systems used in industrial, academic, and medical research.

Tracor Northern does some $27 million worth of business annually and has 275 employees in Middleton, with another 65 in sales and service offices around the country. It is a division of Tracor Inc., a $710 million-a-year conglomorate specializing in work for the defense department.

In 1989, Tracor Northern announced an exciting new product that had been five years in the making: an automated digital electronic microscope, or ADEM. Tracor Northern became only the third U.S. manufacturer of ADEM, a $250,000 machine that ties together a computer and scanning electron microscope.

At the opposite end of Madison, northeast of the city and a 12-minute drive from the Dane County Airport, lies Sun Prairie, a fast-growing city that in the mid-1980s tossed its hat into the business park derby.

Sun Prairie's population increased nearly 500 percent in the 25 years between 1961 and 1986, rising from 2,500 to approximately 14,000. The community has equally ambitious hopes in the area of economic growth.

In 1987, John Bogle, president of the Sun Prairie Industrial Development Corporation, told *In Business* magazine, "We think we can get $100 million of new development in 10 to 20 years. That's perhaps a little ambitious, but we've got a good start."

Sun Prairie's dream of a first-class business park began in 1983, with a proposal by a seven-member mayoral ad hoc committee investigating strategies for industrial revitalization. In February 1984, the committee members formed and became directors of the Industrial Development Corporation—in the belief that many firms would rather deal with a private corporation than a municipal government or even a chamber of commerce.

It worked. In three years the group developed 70 of the 140 acres available at the park's County Highway N-U.S. Highway 151 location. The first firm to build in the park was a longtime Sun Prairie firm, Diesel Injection Service, which had been planning an expansion outside of Sun Prairie but changed its plans when the park site became available.

The Sun Prairie park was aided by the city council establishing it as a tax incremental financing (TIF) district; this was also the way another Greater Madison community,

If a Madison resident is ever on a television game show and is asked to name the original signers of the constitution, all he or she need do is tick off the names of downtown streets. Thirty-six of 37 are represented on Madison street signs—only George Read of Delaware was omitted. (Doty either didn't like him or, more likely, simply forgot him.) If the downtown street names and some "pioneer buildings" provide Madison a link to the past, the abundant new construction downtown is setting a foundation for the future. The 1980s will likely be looked upon as the decade when Madison's downtown got a facelift and a new look.

One should actually go back just a little farther, to March 1974, at the opening of the First Wisconsin Plaza on Pickney Street on the Capitol Square. The "glass bank," as everyone refers to it, is a physically stunning office complex and one of the state's most prestigious business addresses.

In July 1981 ground was broken on the Capitol Centre, a $30-million multifaceted project located three blocks northwest of the Square. Completed in 1983, the Capitol Centre consists of two 16-story high-rises, three three-story townhouses, underground parking, a large above-ground parking ramp, two landscape plazas, a freestanding commercial building, and a grocery store.

Directly across the street from the Capitol Centre is the building many people feel is Madison's most daring example of modern architecture. Surprisingly enough, it's a courthouse. The new federal courthouse for the western district of Wisconsin was designed by noted Madison architect Kenton Peters. Completed in October 1984 at a cost of $5.9 million, the federal courthouse has a shiny blue, futuristic exterior which people seem to either love or hate. In any case, it rarely goes unnoticed.

By the time the new courthouse opened in 1984, an eye-opening number of other downtown projects were going forward. Among the most significant was a $5.6-million renovation of the Tenney Plaza, 10 stories of offices located adjacent to the First Wisconsin Plaza on the Capitol Square.

The Tenney project included parking, as did a $4-million renovation of a professional office building

Stoughton, engineered a downtown landscape-revitalization program in the late 1980s.

Located about 15 miles south of Madison on Highway 51, the Stoughton Chamber of Commerce decided the area had been kept a secret for too long and in 1987 established a retail acquisition committee which helped get the TIF district established in Stoughton's downtown—a plan that concentrated on preserving the historical flavor of the area.

In the spring of 1988, Stoughton attracted a Walmart store, with 82,000 square feet of retail space and some 100 new jobs. There are future plans for a restaurant or bank to complete the complex.

The "only Waunakee in the world" is another Greater Madison community looking to bust out economically. Located just north of Madison, this town of 2,500 has been touting itself as an industrial site.

In July 1987, Waunakee Chamber of Commerce President Paul Maggio told *In Business* magazine, "I think Waunakee has a great potential as an industrial site for companies, just because of the proximity to the Interstate and the airport."

In the 1980s Waunakee attracted several industries, including Scientific Protein Labs, Germania Dairy Automation, and the Nord Gear Corporation, which manufactures speed reducers and gearmotors for general industry. The community's largest private employer is Marshall Erdman, a manufacturer of cabinetry and prefabricated components for medical buildings, which employs 175 people in its 450,000-square-foot plant.

One final Greater Madison community, Cambridge, is seeking to develop a unique economic niche. Located some 20 miles from Madison on Highway 18, Cambridge is selling itself as a tourist town, creating an image of quaint, historic buildings and a bustling arts and crafts community. In the late 1980s Cambridge undertook a refurbishing effort that included restoring downtown buildings to the original Victorian designs. New specialty shops included a blacksmith, two potters, and a handcrafted jewelry store.

The Cambridge Chamber of Commerce president told *In Business*, "I think we're in the embryo stage of developing into a specialized tourist community."

The sports bug bites
the entire Madison
area every spring.
Photo by Bruce Fritz

on another corner of the Square, at 100 North Hamilton Street, and the Munz Building, a first-class office complex overlooking Lake Monona on East Wilson Street.

These and other projects with their own parking facilities have helped ease the parking crunch that plagued downtown Madison for years. City residents have gradually come to the realization that it is no longer impossible to park downtown; in fact it's fairly easy.

The most recent, and perhaps the most impressive office and retail complex in the downtown, is Manchester Place, completed in 1987 and located on the Square off Mifflin Street. Taking its name from the old Manchester's department store once located there, Manchester Place is a 10-story, $12.8-million complex which many naysayers doubted would be built. It was, however, and it provides further proof of the downtown's economic vitality.

As the 1980s drew to a close, the hottest debate involving Madison's downtown was provoked by a proposed convention center. Originating from the office of Madison Mayor Joe Sensenbrenner in December

1985, the proposal was targeted for the north side of the Capitol Square on land being vacated by the Madison Area Technical College.

Over the next several years, however, the proposal sat on a back burner while considerable controversy grew around it. While almost everyone agreed Madison could use a first-class convention center downtown, there was less agreement on *where* downtown it should be located, how much it should cost, and who should pay for it. The good news at this writing is that the polemics seem finally to have been set aside, the various factions are at least talking, and there is renewed hope that a convention center will indeed be built in the central city. There is still a long way to go, however, to make it a reality.

With all the talk of offices, government, and housing, it's important to remember there exists downtown a street teeming with the vitality of the retail trade, a street that also serves to link the State Capitol and the University of Wisconsin-Madison campus, a street that is legendary around the State of Wisconsin and the entire Midwest—State Street.

It was originally an extension of King Street, but was renamed in 1855 by an act of the state legislature. In its early years and into the middle of this century, State Street was a mix of private homes, university properties (on the end opposite the Capitol), and small, owner-operated shops.

As the university grew and more students came to Madison, State Street began to assume a new identity. It became a gathering place for an interesting assortment of students, musicians, poets, activists, actors, and businesspeople who delighted in the informal ambience. One of the more intriguing aspects of State Street is how it can seem simultaneously active and laid-back.

Before long, merchants caught on, and State Street today bustles with ethnic restaurants, wonderful new and used bookstores, music shops, clothing stores, crafts shops—a true rainbow coalition of retail.

A turning point for State Street came in the 1970s when the decision was made to close the street to

This view of the city from Lake Mendota is suggestive of an exotic port city vista. Photo by Bruce Fritz

traffic, creating the State Street Mall. The two blocks nearest the university campus had been closed first, in 1972, and the Memorial Library Mall had become a wonderful milling place for students who enjoyed the cool fountain that flowed in summer and the artists and crafts people who sold their wares in all but the coldest weather.

People wondered: Why not make the entire street a pedestrian mall? A few years later it was, and State Street's unique charm was assured. As both a physical and spiritual extension of the Capitol Square, it is a place to shop, people-watch, and delight in Madison's diversity.

Almost as much as the Capitol, State Street is a symbol of Madison's downtown, and indeed, of the city as a whole. It is where state government, the university, and the private sector quite literally come together. It's an economic and a social phenomenon.

What the University of Wisconsin brings Madison and the downtown in particular can be measured on State Street. The 100 specialty shops and restaurants that line the State Street Mall count on UW's 44,000 students (and 20,000 employees) for their survival.

A concentrated example of the big economic story of Madison's last decade—one that will be discussed later in this book—is the growing UW-private sector partnership in economic development.

But it's also more than that, much more. UW-Madison infuses the downtown and the city with a vibrant spirit. Simply put, life is richer here because of the presence of an outstanding university. Once again, you can see it on State Street; the 3,600 foreign students from 125 countries lend the street a cosmopolitan feel. Just off State Street, sipping a beer on the terrace of the Memorial Union, people-watching as the gentle waves of Lake Mendota lap the shoreline, you might think for a moment you were in some exotic port city.

But no. You're simply lucky enough to be enjoying life downtown in a city where doing so is a vital, varied, and thoroughly rewarding experience.

CHAPTER THREE

The Enterprising Spirit

I n 1987 *Inc.* magazine, the highly respected national business publication, let the country in on a secret Madisonians had known for several years: namely that Madison's economy is among the most vibrant in the country, mixing government, education, and private sector opportunities in a way that make it an attractive and exciting place to do business.

Inc. named Madison as one of the 50 "most vibrant and fastest growing cities in the United States," based on data collected from 1982 to 1986 regarding job creation, corporate start-ups, and business growth. The 50 cities, the magazine said, have in common "healthy systems of education, communication and transportation, complemented by local governments committed to economic development."

That commitment and the spirit of cooperation that exists in Madison today were exemplified in the fall of 1988 when Dane

There are more than 3,000 farms in Dane County, according to the Wisconsin Agriculture Reporting Service. The region is ranked among the top 10 counties in the nation in value of farm products. Photo by Bruce Fritz

**Madison has long
been known as the
trade center of a rich
agricultural region.
Photo by Bruce Fritz**

County Executive Richard Phelps announced the first Dane County "economic summit" to craft a common agenda for the county's economic future. The summit meetings brought together over 100 business, community, labor, and educational leaders from all across Dane County. The coordinating committee for the summit included University of Wisconsin-Madison Chancellor Donna Shalala and recently retired Oscar Mayer executive Jerry Hiegel, proving that in Madison cooperation between the university, government, and private sector is in full blossom.

As a result, Madison's economy heading into the 1990s and beyond has never been stronger. The foundation of that success lies in the economic diversity of the city; long known as the trade center of a rich agricultural region, Madison today is home to business and industry of all kinds, from manufacturing giants to an array of companies on the cutting edge of high technology. The city is teeming with retail malls, and is a home to insurance companies.

As Ron Shaffer, a professor of agricultural economics at UW-Madison, told *Madison Magazine* in 1988, "The economy in Dane County is diversified." Shaffer pointed to studies he had conducted which showed that from 1978 to 1987 there had been a net increase of 26,100 jobs in the local economy. Just under half of them, or 11,700, were in service industries, but there were gains across the board: 2,300 new jobs in manufacturing, 6,800 in retailing, and 5,300 in the financial service fields.

A colleague of Shaffer, UW-Madison School of Business Associate Dean William Strang, told the magazine, "One of the nice things about Madison is that we're not dependent on any one entity for too large a portion of our base. Lots of different companies contribute in smaller pieces, so all our eggs aren't in one basket."

Madison has never suffered the cyclical ups and downs that affect the economics of many cities nationally and particularly in the Midwest. Unemployment in Dane County in the late 1980s was virtually nonexistent. Through the late summer months of 1988 the average unemployment rate was 2.5 percent, down from 3.4 percent in June 1987. From 1982 to 1988, Madison's economy grew at a rate of 5.9 percent annually.

The gently rolling terrain of Dane County is ideal for many types of livestock and crops. Photo by Bruce Fritz

RIGHT: American Family Insurance is the nation's 12th-largest property and casualty insurance company, and is Dane County's second-largest private employer. Photo by Brad Crooks

BELOW: One multifaceted insurance giant headquartered in Madison is CUNA—the Credit Union National Association. Its growth has encompassed a wide array of insurance and financial services. Photo by Brent Nicastro

That enviable record is due in part to the high number of government and university jobs in Madison. In 1988 the State of Wisconsin was Dane County's largest employer, providing 41,300 jobs. UW-Madison was next with 19,204 employees (22,259 counting the UW Hospital and Clinics), followed by the United States Government (3,623), the Madison School District (2,756), Oscar Mayer Foods Corporation (2,600), the City of Madison (2,250), American Family Insurance (2,100), Meriter-Madison General Hospital (1,850), Dane County Government (1,601), and Madison Area Technical College (1,600).

A more general employment breakdown shows that of the 213,000 people employed in Dane County in June 1987, 57,800 worked for the government; 42,000 were in the service industry; 43,300 in wholesale and retail trade; 22,400 in manufacturing; 6,700 in transportation, communication, electric, gas, and sanitary service; and 5,900 in contract construction. Dane County had a total of 7,456 employing establishments in 1987.

The low unemployment rate is just one of many "quality of life" factors that make Madison such an ideal place to live and work. A recent national survey listed Madison as the second "least stressful" city in the country among cities of comparable population.

Some of that may be due to the city's consistently low crime rate. The FBI's 1986 uniform crime report found that based on incidents per 100,000 population, Madison has the lowest murder and assault rate and the second lowest rape, robbery, and arson rates in cities of similar size.

It's not surprising, then, to learn Madison is a growing city. Its 1987 population of 176,053 was up from 170,616 in 1980. Growth in Dane County is even more rapid. The county's 1980 population of 323,545 was projected to reach 357,923 by 1990.

The spirit of growth is reflected in the city's major employers. Nearly every one of Madison's largest companies announced local expansions in the past few years.

No plans are more ambitious, or show more of a commitment to Madison, than those of American Family Insurance, the nation's 12th-largest property and casualty insurance company. American Family has been headquartered in Madison for more than 60 years and is Dane County's second-largest private employer.

With their planned expansion, they may soon be the largest. In 1988 American Family paid $2.5 million for 753 acres of land in the town of Burke, just northeast of Madison beyond the intersection of U.S. Highway 51 and Interstate 90-94. A short time later, the city council voted to annex that land to Madison.

The company had simply outgrown their longtime facility on East Washington Avenue. The expansion, slated to begin in 1989, was budgeted at between $40 million and $60 million, and will include the American Family headquarters on 157 acres, a 133-acre office park, and a 56-acre commercial district. It will be a fitting home base for a company that boasts a total of 5,600 employees with operations in 12 states and assets totaling $4.5 billion.

The expansion does not just involve facilities. By 1997 American Family projects it will employ 3,402 people in Dane County, and by the year 2010 local employment at American Family may reach 10,643.

The state of Wisconsin, and Madison in particular, is a haven for insurance companies. A 1983 national study listed Madison as second only to Hartford in the number of per capita insurance company home offices.

There are a number of reasons for this, including the excellent reputation of Wisconsin's insurance commission, along with the presence in Madison of the University of Wisconsin. In a 1983 interview with *Madison Magazine*, Dennis Carlson, a vice president at Rural Insurance in Madison, elaborated on that point. "I think Wisconsin has one of the best insurance commissions in the country," he said. "Working with them is very satisfying. They are highly regarded nationally. You'll hear statements like, 'Well, if the Wisconsin insurance department thinks this is right, it must be okay.'"

Carlson continued, "I also think the

University of Wisconsin has one of the finest actuarial science programs in its School of Business as you'll find anywhere in the country. Companies in Madison and across the state get a lot of graduates out of that program."

One multifaceted insurance giant headquartered in Madison is CUNA—the Credit Union National Association. CUNA was founded in the 1930s by the leaders of the credit union movement with the motto, "not for profit, not for charity, but for service." Its subsequent growth has encompassed a wide array of insurance and financial services but it has remained headquartered in Madison on Mineral Point Road on the city's West Side.

CUNA is actually an umbrella title that covers several different organizations housed in three separate buildings referred to as the World Credit Union Center, with total employment of around 2,000. Of those, the Credit Union National Association employs 430 and serves as the trade association of nearly 90 percent of the nation's credit unions, serving 18,000 credit unions and 52 million members in all. Another six organizations employing 1,545 people make up

Oscar Mayer is the nation's eighth-largest meat company and the nation's top producer of wieners, lunch meats, and bacon.
Photo by Brad Crooks

A happy youngster is enjoying a romp amid the traditional roadside display of autumnal gourds for sale along Highway 14. Photo by Bruce Fritz

the CUNA Mutual Insurance Group, which provides insurance to credit unions and their members along with various other financial and investment services.

In 1987 CUNA finished a $14-million expansion project, and it continues to be one of Madison's fastest growing and vibrant employers. In its 1980 annual report, CUNA Mutual listed assets of $565 million—by 1985 their assets topped one billion dollars.

Manufacturing is also important in Madison. Over 22,000 people are employed in Madison-area manufacturing. The number one manufacturer, the largest private employer in Dane County, is the Oscar Mayer Foods Corporation. Oscar Mayer is the nation's eighth-largest meat company and is the country's top producer of wieners, lunch meats, and bacon. Oscar Mayer's sales top $2 billion annually.

There was some concern about the 2,600 jobs at Oscar Mayer when the company was sold in 1981 to the General Foods Corporation, a subsidiary of Philip Morris. Happily for Madison, General Foods has reaffirmed Oscar Mayer's commitment to the city, evidenced by a $7-million addition in 1986.

That addition came in conjunction with the transfer to Madison of executives from Oscar Mayer's Louis Rich division. In 1979, presciently recognizing the nation's move away from red meat, Oscar Mayer acquired Louis Rich, a manufacturer of turkey and chicken. More recently, Oscar Mayer acquired a seafood company, and while the meatpacking industry as a whole endures troubled times, Oscar Mayer remains healthy.

Madison has been fortunate in that its most important corporate citizens have almost uniformly retained their vitality, or if that vitality had been lost, it has been regained with a vengeance.

Nowhere is this better evidenced than in the recent history of the Rayovac Company, a Madison-based manufacturer of batteries for industrial and home use. Rayovac had been in Madison since 1906, but by 1982 the company was spinning its wheels, a distant third in its market share and losing $20 million annually.

Late in 1982, however, the company was purchased by a Pennsylvania native who had earned an MBA at the University of Wisconsin 25 years before. Tom Pyle had always liked Madison, and with the active help of his wife, Judy, he came back to the city and recharged Rayovac in just a few short years.

Within six months, the Pyles—Tom serving as president and CEO, Judy as vice president in charge of marketing—redesigned the look of the company and introduced a new product, the Work-horse flashlight, into the "premium" market. By the end of the Pyles' first year Rayovac was breaking even; in year two it turned a healthy profit.

In 1986 Rayovac's comeback was completed when it moved into a new, multimillion-dollar corporate headquarters off the West Beltline Highway in Madison. By the end of 1987 Rayovac's sales were at $270 million annually, and a survey of Wisconsin's top 100 private companies, conducted by a Milwaukee accounting firm, ranked Rayovac 12th in the state in total annual sales.

Interestingly, the company ranked 15th on that exclusive list is also a Madison company, but it's a retailer, not a manufacturer. American TV and Appliance is recognized nationally as a retailing phenomenon, having grown from a small, nearly bankrupt television store into a stereo, television, and appliance empire with annual sales in excess of $150 million.

American TV's meteoric rise was largely the work of one man, Len Mattioli, who took over the company from his ailing brother in 1969 and with a series of shrewd marketing moves, including a barrage of outrageous advertisements and giveaways, slowly and surely built his empire. With multiple stores in Madison, Milwaukee, and elsewhere, Mattioli is now regarded as a marketing genius.

American TV and Appliance embodies the vigor and competitive spirit of the Madison retail market. In 1980, according to the U.S. Census Bureau, there were 2,039 retail stores in Dane County, employing 29,021 people. By 1985 there were 2,343 retail stores employing 33,243 people.

It's a growth trend that is continuing. In October 1986 the retail giant Marshall Field's opened a department store in the Hilldale Mall, and in March 1987 a new Boston store opened in the East Towne Mall.

Most of the city's retail malls are thriving. Among the biggest are Hilldale, which in 1988 boasted 100 percent occupancy; East Towne, with a 93 percent occupancy rate; and West Towne, with 90 percent occupancy and a new 12-store food court.

In addition, bustling pockets of retail exist throughout the city. State Street's fun and diverse shops, of

Madison: High-Tech Haven

A 1988 joint study compiled by the City of Madison Community and Development Unit and the Madison Gas and Electric Company found more than 200 firms in the Greater Madison area that can be considered "high tech."

Only 20 percent of the firms are based in manufacturing, the report concluded, with the balance concentrating on computer software and hardware, biotechnology, biomedical research, and other specialties, reflecting the impact of technology transfer from the University of Wisconsin to private sector companies in Madison.

Those kind of statistics back up Madison Chamber of Commerce head Robert Brennan's assertion that the city "is one of the best kept secrets in America" when it comes to technology transfer and high-tech development.

No question, the presence of the UW is the straw that stirs the drink as far as high-tech development in Madison is concerned. David Birch, a nationally recognized expert on job creation, recently commented, "Universities, particularly those that concentrate upon research, are the wellspring of the high-innovation economy . . . Whole new industries spring up around university laboratories."

It was the UW which in 1988 helped Madison make the short list as a potential site for Sematech, the semiconductor consortium (consisting of 13 major high-tech companies) which at the time was looking for a home and promising 600 well-paid specialized jobs in the bargain.

Madison made the final five but Sematech chose to locate in Austin, Texas. While disappointed, Madison officials felt their Sematech initiative was a success in that it allowed the city to showcase itself to the country, publicizing the strengths that have helped draw other high-tech companies to the area.

One of the most successful high-tech firms in the Madison area is Agracetus, a Middleton-based company specializing in genetic engineering. Agracetus is a joint venture of the Cetus Corporation of California and W.R. Grace of New York City. The company, which came to Madison in 1981, is a leader nationally in three areas: genetically modified plants, microbial crop treatment, and veterinary pharmaceuticals.

(continued on next page)

East Towne Mall is
one of the many Madi-
son retail malls that
are thriving. Photo by
Brad Crooks

course, draw shoppers from all over the Midwest. There is Monroe Street on the city's near West Side, Williamson Street on the East Side, and many, many more—a March 1988 survey by the Greater Madison Chamber of Commerce identified 76 retail malls and shopping areas in Madison alone.

Quite apart from the glitz of the shopping malls, but equally important to the economic health of Dane County, is agriculture. Close to one-sixth of all farms in Wisconsin are in the Greater Madison trade area, and Dane County is ranked among the top 10 counties in the nation in value of farm products.

There are 3,170 farms located in Dane County, according to the Wisconsin Agriculture Reporting Service. That translates into 620,000 acres, or 78 percent of the total acreage in the county. Leading agricultural products include field crops such as corn, alfalfa, and oats; poultry and eggs; meat animals such as cattle and hogs; and vegetables and specialty crops.

Though Dane County suffered with the rest of the Midwest through the drought of 1988, generally the weather—spring, summer, and fall—and the gently roll-

Russ Smestad, vice president of Agracetus, told *Madison Magazine* in February 1989 that Agracetus is a major player not only nationally, but internationally.

"We're the leader in cotton and the only company in the world genetically engineering soybeans," Smestad said.

By applying recombinant DNA to crops such as cotton, soybeans, and corn, quality and yield can be improved as the crops are made resistant to disease and insects.

In 1986, Agracetus became the first firm to grow gene-spliced plants outdoors, and it also developed a caterpillar-killing cotton plant currently undergoing testing in the South.

Another Madison company, the Promega Corporation, is recognized around the world as a leader in molecular biology research, including

nucleic acid probes and restrictions and the modifying of DNA enzymes.

The University Research Park, begun in 1984 on 325 acres about three miles west of the campus in Madison, has helped solidify the city's reputation as a high-tech haven. Eight companies with some 500 employees located in the park in its first four years.

The January 1987 issue of *High Technology* magazine featured the University Research Park in a piece titled "Little Silicon Valleys," in which Madison was mentioned along with Ann Arbor and Indianapolis as an "aspiring high-tech mecca."

The magazine listed four elements necessary for any aspiring "Silicon Valley": a scientifically-oriented university, technological parks, money, and a cultural climate

conducive to the life-style and business needs of risk-taking entrepreneurs.

Two firms located at the University Research Park were specifically featured in the *High Technology* article: Persoft, which makes emulation software, and Warzyn Engineering, which is involved with surface water quality and waste disposal.

In April 1989, a major new partnership between Madison Gas and Electric, the University Research Park, and the private sector in Madison occurred with the opening of the Madison Gas and Electric Innovation Center at the University Research Park. MG&E made a $400,000 investment to subsidize the center for the first three years. The Innovation Center occupies half of a 20,000-square-foot building on Science

ing terrain are ideal for farming. The absolute temperature range may seem a little scary—from 107 degrees Fahrenheit to -37 degrees Fahrenheit—but the averages are far more pleasant: the summer average is 68 degrees and the winter, 20 degrees.

High-technology businesses may be the fastest growing segment of the Madison economy. From 1980 to 1988 employment in the high-tech field increased in Madison at a rate of 8.5 percent a year. In January 1987 Madison Mayor Joe Sensenbrenner told *Madison Magazine*, "We are drawing on our educational base," and pointed to 30 high-tech companies in the city which employed approximately 2,700 people.

No question, UW-Madison's presence has helped the city work toward becoming the "Silicon Valley of the Midwest." In 1984 UW-Madison established a Research Park on the city's West Side with the specific goal of attracting high-technology-oriented tenants.

Located on 320 acres at the intersection of Mineral Point Road and Whitney Way, the University Research Park quickly picked up two tenants—Warzyn Engineering and Persoft, the latter a computer soft-ware firm started by three former UW-Madison computer scientists.

Growth of the University Research Park slowed for a time, but new tenants were gradually added, and in 1988 the Hospital Corporation of America signed a 70-year, $1,365,000 lease and broke ground on a new psychiatric hospital in the park. Also in 1988 the University Research Park received a $20,000 grant from Wisconsin Bell to establish a fiber optics communication link between the campus and the park, allowing tenants of the park to interact more easily with UW-Madison faculty and the UW computer network.

At about the same time the University Research Park was developing, a 408-acre research and business park, to be developed privately, was introduced and slated for development just outside the city at Old Sauk and Gammon roads. The Old Sauk Trails Park, as it is called, came together even more quickly than the University Research Park. In 1988 the Old Sauk Park scored a real coup when RMT, a Madison-based environmental consulting firm, announced plans for a $7-million, 74,000-square-foot office and laboratory on Drive in the park.

The center's goal is to provide high-quality, below-market-cost office and laboratory space and equipment, as well as on-site clerical and management assistance, to fledgling companies in high-tech businesses like computer software and biotechnology.

Madison had an existing—and successful, with 75 percent occupancy—"business incubator" at 210 N. Bassett Street downtown, but the MG&E facility offers the extra dimension of laboratory space.

National surveys have shown that new businesses located in an incubator or Innovation Center-type facility have success rates of 75 percent versus the average of 50 percent among all start-up ventures. The studies also indicate that close to nine out of 10 such companies relocate in the same city upon leaving the incubator.

One area where Madison, and, indeed, the state of Wisconsin and the entire Midwest, have had a problem is in securing enough venture capital for high-tech development. Entrepreneurism is relatively new to the Midwest, and risk-taking has never been a high priority of those holding the purse strings of old Midwestern money. For new technology businesses to really take off, that must change.

"Not all high-tech companies are self-sufficient," Agracetus' Russ Smestad told *Madison Magazine* in 1989, adding that his firm has often had to look outside the state for venture capital. "For smaller firms, [high-tech] can be very financially intensive, because longer timetables require greater capital outlay.

"Ongoing research costs money," Smestad continued. "Without a commercial product, a company may be hard put to match a long-term development timetable."

Mind-sets are beginning to change. In 1988, Robert Brennan of the Madison Chamber of Commerce developed the Wisconsin Information Network (WIN), which attempts to match the needs of entrepreneurs with adequate funding while generally raising the profile of high-tech development.

It's a slow process, but it's working. At the request of Wisconsin Governor Tommy Thompson, the WIN program was expanded outside of Madison to encompass the entire state.

The temperature range
in Madison may seem
a bit extreme—from
107 degrees to -37 de-
grees Fahrenheit—but
the averages are quite
pleasant. Photo by
Bruce Fritz

seven acres in the park.

At the time of the announcement, RMT employed 180 people in Madison. A spokesman told the *Wisconsin State Journal* that over the next three years the company anticipated adding 20 to 25 technical employees as well as 50 engineers, industrial hygienists, chemists, and hydrogeologists.

While the research parks and the big tenants are certainly good for the city, it is the entrepreneurial spirit the high-technology industry symbolizes that may be the most meaningful for Madison. All over the city, people are bursting with enterprising new ideas.

They've been helped by a series of "Venture Fairs" sponsored by the Greater Madison Chamber of Commerce. The fairs began in 1984, using the University of Michigan venture fairs as a model. The idea was to bring fledgling entrepreneurs together with venture capitalists in the hope of creating, or expanding, new businesses. In Michigan about 15 entrepreneurs are showcased and one or two receive funding.

Madison did better right from the start. The first fair matched 40 percent of the entrepreneurs with venture capitalists; the 1985 fair did even better, with 6 of 13 entrepreneurs getting funding. The 1985 fair was held at the Concourse Hotel in Madison, and the 13 entrepreneurs made their pitch to about 40 venture capitalists; ideas included a children's book publishing company and a sophisticated visual prosthetic device for the blind.

The Venture Fairs have grown each year. One recent example of a company receiving funding from the fairs is Persoft, located in the University Research Park. Persoft made its presentation at the 1986 fair, and in 1987 the company received $2.5 million from a Chicago-based venture capital firm. Persoft specializes in writing and marketing communications software that links personal computers with larger mainline computers.

Dozens of success stories have come out of the fairs. Promega, a Madison firm which manufactures and sells enzymes to biologists, saw sales increase 2,000 percent in the four years since making its first Venture Fair appearance in 1984. In 1987 Promega was recognized as one of the fastest growing companies in the nation by *Inc.* magazine.

It's increasingly easy for venture capitalists and other travelers to get to Madison. The Dane County Regional Airport underwent a significant expansion and remodeling project, which, when completed in 1986,

gave the city a first-class facility.

The number of airlines flying into Madison changes with the prevailing winds of takeovers and acquisitions, but as of 1989 eight commercial flyers—American Eagle, Midwest Express, TWA, United, Northwest, United Express, Air Toronto, and Midway Connection—regularly flew to Madison, making an estimated 80 takeoffs and landings daily. In 1987 more than 900,000 passengers traveled through the Dane County Regional Airport.

Madison is also served by four bus companies, five air cargo companies, more than 40 common carrier truck lines, and four railroads. Two of Wisconsin's three interstate highways (I-90 and I-94) pass through Madison, and the city is also the hub of five U.S. highways and two state highways. Travelers to Minneapolis, Chicago, and Milwaukee can do so on a single highway.

For Madisonians, the fall of 1988 saw the completion of a 25-year dream: an expansion of Highways 12-18 from I-90 to John Nolen Drive. Commonly called the Beltline, this expanded highway will facilitate travel from I-90—the major Chicago to Milwaukee route—to both Madison's downtown and West Side.

Travelers will find some 19 hotels and motels in Madison with 100 or more rooms (as of 1988), and another 14 with 31 to 99 rooms.

The convention and visitors industry is an important one for the city. While debate continues on whether or not to build a major new convention center downtown, the existing industry is thriving.

In 1982 the Recreation Resources Center of the University of Wisconsin-Extension prepared a fact sheet of 1981 statistics for the Greater Madison Visitor and Convention Bureau. The results were eye-opening.

In 1981 some 950,000 visitors to Madison stayed overnight a total of 1.9 million days and generated over $95 million in the city. Madison lodging establishments made over $17 million from the overnight guests, eating and drinking places more than $51 million, service stations over $10 million, and amusement and recreation businesses more than $5 million, with another $9.9 million going for general merchandise. The City of Madison itself received over one million dollars in direct room taxes from overnight visitors in 1981.

Those big numbers shouldn't be surprising. As home to the University of Wisconsin and the state capital, Madison is a natural destination for travelers. People enjoy visiting, just as they enjoy living and working here.

Madison is a natural
destination for many
travelers. Photo by
Bruce Fritz

CHAPTER FOUR

The Service Sector

I n 1946, writing about the most colorful cities in America, the *Saturday Evening Post* referred to Madison as "a fortuitous greenhouse for the transplantation and ripening of youth. It is a town where the battle lines are drawn against such ageless enemies of man as ignorance and disease. A town where Lincoln could have grown up in harmony, where Galileo could have spoken his mind and where Demosthenes could have been mayor."

More than four decades later the magazine's lively description of Madison still applies. In the areas of education and health care, anchored by the University of Wisconsin and the UW Hospital and Clinics, Madison is in the forefront nationally. On both the state and local levels Madison enjoys a reputation for clean government, and in recent years the government has reached out to embrace the private sector with a variety of services designed to make doing business here more rewarding.

When it is in your own backyard, an institution such as the University of Wisconsin can often be underappreciated and taken for granted. That's why it's occasionally nice to be reminded of the sterling reputa-

Madison is in the national forefront of health care and education. Photo by Bruce Fritz

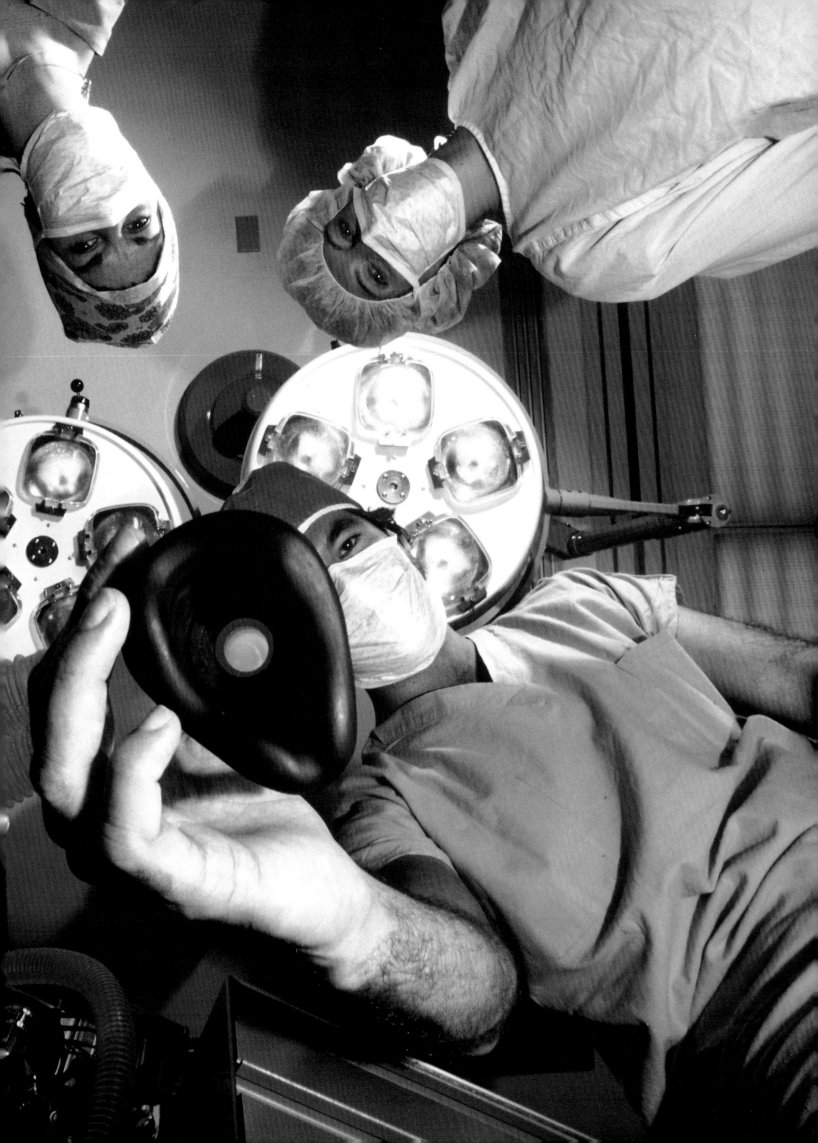

tion UW enjoys around the world.

UW-Madison has ranked among the top 10 universities in the United States in nearly all studies of academic excellence in this century. Combining the results of seven major studies conducted since 1925, a University of Pennsylvania professor, writing for the June 1983 issue of *Change* magazine, ranked UW-Madison fourth in the nation, behind Harvard, UC-Berkeley, and Yale, and tied with the University of Chicago. A 1983 "Assessment of Research-Doctorate Programs in the United States" listed UW-Madison as tied for eighth in reputation for scholarly quality and second on the basis of faculty publications.

Students over the years at the UW have included Eudora Welty, Marjorie Kinnan Rawlings, and Charles Lindbergh. Vitamin B was discovered at UW, the round silo was invented there, the first gene synthesized, and the first social security legislation drafted.

UW's 1987 enrollment of 43,368 is one of the largest in the nation. Some 4,000 courses are offered in 130 departments. The UW library system boasts four million volumes in 22 locations, all of which are open to the public. Students at UW are well equipped to appreciate that wealth of knowledge: one-third of incoming freshmen rank in the top 10 percent of their high school graduating class.

It's hardly necessary to point out the financial contribution UW makes to the city. A university-sponsored study released in the mid-1980s showed that spending by UW-Madison, its employees, students, and visitors, is worth $1.4 billion a year to Madison and Dane County. Visitors to the campus spend $139.9 million. Clothing stores realize $33 million, while restaurants and taverns gain $81 million. UW also spends $46 million a year locally on supplies, equipment, services, and construction. The annual UW budget is more than $920 million.

The true drawing card for UW, and what really sets such impressive economic wheels in motion, is the quality of the faculty. Three UW professors won Nobel Prizes for their work while on the faculty. Seven Nobels have been earned by former students or faculty members. Six have won the prestigious National Medal of Science. Fifty members of the UW faculty are in the National Academies of Science, Engineering, and Education.

Many on the faculty are vigorously involved in research. Indeed, UW-Madison ranks third in the nation in research spending. In 1988 some 5,000 separate research projects were ongoing and attracting more than $230 million into Madison annually, supporting 3,290 full- and part-time employees.

An increasing amount of that research funding was provided by what in the past would have been a most unlikely source: business and industry. For years, in Madison and elsewhere, businesspeople and academia held one another at arm's length.

That changed, and rather dramatically, in the early 1980s. As the nation pulled out of a recession, the universities and the private sector sensed they could help one another; in fact, they *needed* each other. Writing in *Florida Trend* magazine, economist R. Thomas Powers observed, "The top performers coming out of the recession are areas [with] a university . . . By figuring out creative applications for high technology, these universities are becoming the 'water wheel' of the new economy."

From 1982-1983 to 1986-1987, business and corporate contributions toward research at UW-Madison nearly doubled, from $8.3 million to $16.4 million. In September 1988 UW-Madison engineering dean John Bollinger told the *Milwaukee Sentinel* that his college alone had about 170 privately funded research projects under way at any given time, along with about twice that many government-sponsored projects.

Bollinger also told the *Sentinel* that businesses pay anywhere from $20,000 to more than one million dollars for a research project, which will generally last between two and three years. As an example, IBM might provide a $50,000 grant for a particular professor to determine how to improve the production of computer chips. All research at UW-Madison is published, though a sponsoring business gets updated along the way and so receives a competitive edge.

While the university-private sector partnership has only recently come into full blossom, the University-Industry Research Program (UIR) was actually established in 1963. In an August 1985 interview with Madison's *In Business* magazine, UIR's Executive Director Norbert Hildebrand called the program a "window into the University," helping transfer the results of research at the UW into the industrial and economic mainstream of the state.

UIR was responsible for coordinating the industrial consortia now active on the UW-Madison campus. (A consortium consists of a group of companies that contribute support to a faculty research program, the results of which are shared equally by the members.)

Such a resource can profoundly affect Wisconsin industry. In the early 1980s, foundries in the state were in trouble because they were having problems controlling waste, and they lacked the research capability to solve the problem. A consortium of Wisconsin's foundries was put together, and with the help of UW's cast metals program, a design program and software package were developed within two years.

UIR also conducts seminars, bringing together representatives of industry and the university to discuss mutual research interests. In association with the Wendt Engineering Library, UIR provides a one-stop scientific and technical information center called the Information Services Division (ISD). In 1985 alone the ISD processed more than 18,000 inquiries from more than 650 firms (one-third from Wisconsin, the rest from 34 states and 6 foreign countries). The inquiries often involve requests for the latest information on patenting trends and patent searches. The UW also publishes a 100-page Directory of University Resources, which helps businesses learn what is available to them throughout the UW system.

Like the university, state government in Madison has taken an active role in helping business. The Department of Development (DOD) is the state agency most engaged in providing a variety of services to businesses. Throughout the 1980s the DOD established programs to help state businesses, including a permit center to assist in obtaining state agency permits, a "mentor program" in which Wisconsin firms with international trade experience provide free assistance to state firms seeking foreign markets, a Quick Start program that provides matching grant money to train employees of companies expanding into new technologies, and the Technology Development Fund, money granted to joint business-university projects.

The growing partnership in Madison of government, the private sector, and the university community was recognized in 1988 when Governor Tommy Thompson announced that Sematech, the research consortium of the U.S. semiconductor industry, had selected UW-Madison as one of 10 U.S. universities to be "Centers of Excellence."

That year Madison had been actively involved in recruiting a new Sematech research facility to Madison. While Austin, Texas was eventually selected

TOP: These UW-Madison students are involved in computer-aided engineering projects. Photo by Bruce Fritz

BOTTOM: A football player studies at the University of Wisconsin-Madison. The university's enrollment of more than 43,000 is one of the largest in the nation. Photo by Bruce Fritz

Students and faculty
can relax on the Uni-
versity's Memorial Un-
ion Terrace. A recent
study indicates that
spending by UW-
Madison, its em-
ployees, students, and
visitors, is worth $1.4
billion a year to Madi-
son and Dane County.
Photo by Bruce Fritz

as the site, Sematech was impressed enough with both the community and UW to commit substantial research dollars to Madison with their "Center for Excellence" award. UW-Madison was singled out for its research program in X-ray lithography, an area of research generally acknowledged to be on the cutting edge of the next generation of computers. "The university's world-renowned resources and capabilities served as the cornerstone of Wisconsin's entire Sematech initiative," Governor Thompson said. "I applaud the university as well as the many other business and government leaders who helped Wisconsin assume a leadership role in the nation's effort to stay competitive in micro-electronics."

Research is also conducted in Madison apart from the university. The city is home to the U.S. Forest Products Laboratory, the only U.S. government lab engaged in wood research. Other nationally recognized research-oriented organizations in Madison include the U.S. Fish and Wildlife Lab, the Space Science and Engineering Center, the Waisman Center of Mental Retardation and Human Development, the Enzyme Institute, the Sea

The large student population becomes apparent during a class change on Bascom Hill at UW-Madison. Photo by Bruce Fritz

A Financial Center

The national deregulation of the financial industry in the 1980s affected Madison in at least two ways: There was an increase in employment in the financial services area and banks and other institutions reflected the national trends of merging and offering a wider array of services.

According to Wisconsin Job Service, employment in the financial service sector in Dane County grew 30.5 percent between 1980 and 1986, to a total of approximately 17,000 jobs.

While insurance companies are included in the "financial services" statistics, the growth indicates how well Dane County banks, savings and loans, and credit unions have adapted to the changing tides of the financial seas heading into the 1990s. Aggressive customer service has become the norm, and because they

prepared for the future, financial institutions in Madison—and throughout Wisconsin—are healthier than many of those in other parts of the country.

Looking to the future, indeed. As one example, in September 1988, Bob Cramer, chief financial officer of Wisconsin's Valley Banks, explained to *Madison Magazine* the growth of Valley—which by then totaled 17 branches and $550 million in assets.

The story goes back to 1978, when a half-dozen Madison area banks—the Bank of Middleton, Bank of Shorewood Hills, American Exchange Bank, Brooklyn State Bank, Monona State Bank, and the Farmers and Merchants Bank of Richland Center—saw the writing on the wall in terms of rising costs and competition which would make independent operation increasingly

Grant Institute, Air Pollution Lab, and the U.S. Department of Agriculture Research Service.

While the UW is the anchor of education in Madison, it is far from alone in promoting academic excellence. Madison Area Technical College (MATC) is one of the Midwest's best vocational colleges, with 87 percent of its graduates finding employment related to their fields within six months of graduation. MATC specializes in associate degrees, vocational diplomas, and apprenticeships. The school had a total enrollment of 33,053 in 1987.

In September 1986 a decade of hard work and discussion came to fruition at MATC with the opening of a second campus in addition to their downtown location, which had suffered from overcrowding. The new MATC-Truax facility, with a price tag of $50 million, is

One-third of incoming freshmen at UW rank in the top 10 percent of their high school graduating class. Here, a student uses a "sip-and-puff" technique to interface with a computer terminal. Photo by Bruce Fritz

difficult. A holding company, Community Banks, Incorporated (CBI), was formed.

Each bank operated as a branch of the others, combining operational resources as well as full-service customer accessibility. Then, in 1986, CBI was acquired by Appleton-based Valley Banks, which had also acquired the United Banks in Madison.

Other than the name change to Valley, Madison customers likely found little changed by all the behind-the-scenes machinations; if anything, the growth provided a more comprehensive financial services network. Valley Bank is currently the fourth-largest holding company in Wisconsin.

"We were worried our customers would be confused or scared off by the merger," Cramer told *Madison Magazine*. "But they so much as said,

'We've been waiting so long for you guys to wise up and get a branch system that we're going to stay with you.'"

According to figures from the state banking commissioner's office, Wisconsin banks were performing well in the late 1980s. For 1988, earnings at state- and federally-chartered banks in Wisconsin climbed to $516 million for the year, up 94 percent from 1987.

"The state's banking industry is in real good shape," Michael Mach, administrator of the commissioner's office, told the *Wisconsin State Journal* in April 1989. "The overall general economy contributed to the good performance, as did a favorable interest rate climate."

The number of mortgages issued in Dane County rose significantly for the first quarter of 1989 as compared to the same three-month

period in 1988, countering a national trend. National sales of existing homes dropped 9.4 percent for January 1989, compared to January 1988. But in Dane County, mortgages were *up* 15 percent, with 1,035 mortgages issued in January 1989 compared to 899 one year earlier.

Home mortgage lending, of course, has long been the backbone of the savings and loan industry. The national savings and loan crisis that rocked the nation in the late 1980s was not felt as severely in Wisconsin. Roughly 500 of the country's 3,000 savings and loans were in trouble by the spring of 1989, but only two were in Wisconsin and neither was in Dane County, according to Wisconsin savings and loan commissioner Harold Lee.

"In Wisconsin, the industry is

located near the Dane County Regional Airport. Its three-story main building covers 700,000 square feet. The new campus boasts 85 classrooms, 107 labs, 29 shops, a cafeteria with seating for more than 600, a 1,000-seat auditorium, and a six-lane, Olympic-size pool.

Edgewood College, a liberal arts college accredited by the North Central Association of Colleges and Secondary Schools, is located on Madison's near West Side, about a mile down Monroe Street from Camp Randall Stadium. Edgewood had a 1987 enrollment of 1,061 and a student-to-faculty ratio of 12:1, with all classes taught by professors.

Madison Area Business College (MBC) is the sixth-oldest school of its type in the country. In September 1980 MBC moved into its current location in the old Spring Harbor Elementary School Building; in 1987, 426 students were enrolled. They benefited from MBC's low student-to-teacher ratio and from the school's outstanding job placement record for graduates, which is often over 90 percent.

Madison's public schools rank near the top nationally. A 1986 study, compiled from California Achievement Tests taken by 11th graders across the country, showed that Madison students ranked in the top 20 percent nationally in mathematics and in the top 25 percent in reading. At the eighth-grade level, Madison pupils scored better than 70 percent of pupils nationally in reading and better than 82 percent in mathematics.

For the fall 1987 term, Madison had 27 public elementary (grades K-5) schools with an enrollment of 10,466, 8 middle (6-8) schools with enrollment of 4,264, and 6 high schools (9-12) with enrollment of 7,136. In addition there were 20 parochial schools in Dane County.

Health care in Madison also rests on a solid base. As an April 1985 article in *Madison Magazine* pointed out: "No matter what criteria are used to measure medical quality—number of physicians, range of specialties, number of hospital beds, the latest in medical technology—Madison is unusually well-endowed."

A 1984 study of physicians showed that Dane County had one doctor for every 264 county residents, compared to one for 462 nationally. Figuring only primary care physicians, the ratio was one for 690,

strong and assets secure," Lee told *Madison Magazine.*

One of the state's major assets is that the majority of Wisconsin savings and loans are chartered by the state, as opposed to federally chartered.

"State-chartered savings and loans," Lee said, "are allowed to react to change quicker, and dealing with state regulators is so much easier than getting involved at the federal level." (State-chartered Wisconsin thrifts, for instance, have had the equivalent of adjustable rate mortgages for 30 years.)

Most states are dominated by federally-chartered savings and loans—Minnesota, for instance, has no state-chartered thrifts. Wisconsin has flipped the equation, with—as of 1987—55 state chartered institutions with 423 branch offices, followed by 20 federally-chartered thrifts with 78 branches.

To attract customers, Dane County savings and loans are also adding services. In 1986, Anchor Savings and Loan, the third largest association in the state with 30 branch offices, formed a service corporation called Anchor Investment Services, which publishes "The Investment Advisor" and helps customers with their financial planning.

Credit unions in Madison and Dane County are also growing. The UW Credit Union—Dane County's largest—competes with banks and thrifts in offering home equity loans.

The UW Credit Union grew 20 percent in membership in 1986 alone, to a total of 57,693 members. It employs 139 people (up 29 percent from 1985) and boasts assets of $145.3 million.

As of 1987, there were 41 credit unions in the country, with the UW Credit Union about twice as big as the second-largest Credit Union National Association.

In 1987, state credit union commissioner Richard Ottow told the *Wisconsin State Journal* that the industry statewide is in good shape, with some 529 state-chartered credit unions. Their financial health is assured by a new law, effective January 1, 1989, requiring all state credit unions to receive insurance by the National Credit Union Insurance Fund.

A UW-Madison student relaxes amid the school's centennial celebration banners.
Photo by Bruce Fritz

compared with about one for 1,146 nationally. Fifty-seven percent of all doctors in the county were board certified, compared with 51 percent nationally.

Dane County has six hospitals, over 100 clinics and urgent care centers, one mental health institute, one center for the developmentally disabled, and five health maintenance organizations.

The crown jewel of Madison's medical community is the University of Wisconsin Hospital and Clinics (UWHC). The authors of the 1986 book, *The Best Hospitals in America,* said this about UWHC: "Its range of medical specialties and services is among the most complete we've come across . . . A major teaching institution, UWHC is a leading center for patient care, biomedical research, education of health professionals, and public service."

The book goes on to give UWHC rave reviews almost across the board, with special mention of the transplant and cancer centers. Of transplants the authors observed:

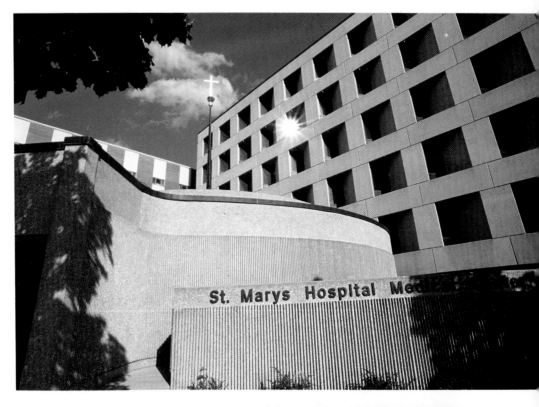

According to the National Transplant Registry, UWHC had the nation's third largest renal transplant center and the second largest pancreas transplant center. The hospital significantly advanced its role as a regional transplant center by incorporating active heart and liver transplantation programs in 1984-85. The state of Wisconsin had the highest per capita rate of organ donation in the nation, and the UWHC procurement team is on twenty-four-hour alert to take calls from any donor hospital or clinic.

The UW Medical School brings in over $40 million annually in public and private grants. Almost half of that money goes to clinical research in areas like oncology (UWHC was one of the first centers to test the cancer drugs interferon and interleukin-2), pediatrics (particularly cystic fibrosis), and ophthalmology (especially in diabetic retinopathy).

In 1987 another Madison hospital, St. Marys, celebrated its 75th anniversary. St. Marys is a 440-bed hospital with a staff of 1,400. It has intensive care units and cardiac laboratories and has placed a special emphasis on maternal-child services.

TOP: St. Marys, a 440-bed hospital with special services for maternity and childcare, recently celebrated its 75th anniversary. Photo by Bruce Fritz

ABOVE: A nurse tends to a very small patient in the special care nursery at Meriter-Madison General Hospital. Photo by Bruce Fritz

Also in 1987 a major business and medical development occurred in Madison when two large hospitals, Madison General and Methodist, merged to form Meriter Hospital (they are now referred to as Meriter-Madison General and Meriter-Methodist).

Allowing for the emotional swings which accompany any merger, the Madison General-Methodist joining has been remarkably successful. In 1988 Meriter executive vice president Terri Potter told the *Wisconsin State Journal* that the hospitals would save an estimated $2 million to $3 million a year in operating costs alone

Madison's television market status was raised in 1988 to 90th in the nation, significant because many national advertisers buy only in the top 100 markets. Photo by Bruce Fritz

without cutting back on patient care. The merger was necessitated by the rapidly changing financial climate in American medicine which has manifested itself in greatly reduced hospital utilization.

The most significant development in Madison health care occurred in 1984 when the State of Wisconsin began offering the health maintenance organization (HMO) option to its employees. HMO consumers, of course, buy memberships instead of insurance, and they or their employer pay a set fee to the HMO in advance—the HMO is then responsible for keeping costs in line.

Half a dozen HMOs sprang up in Madison almost overnight, the most successful of which were—and are—directly linked to large medical groups. The largest is the Dean Medical Center (their HMO is called DeanCare), with a main clinic located on Fish Hatchery Road in Madison. In 1987 that clinic underwent a $6.5-million expansion.

Dean's growth has been extraordinary. As of January 1988 it employed 164 physicians with plans to add another 30. All together the Dean Medical Center employs 700 people and the DeanCare HMO 100 more. With an annual budget of $64 million, Dean provides medical care to almost 171,000 patients.

Another major Madison clinic is the Jackson Clinic, a five-story building on West Washington Avenue in downtown Madison. The fifth floor of the clinic is notable for the presence of the Jackson Foundation, a nationally known, non-profit organization which at any one time is conducting up to 50 drug therapy studies involving 500 patients suffering anything from arthritis to heart disease.

Like the health care business, the media in Madison have grown and changed over the years, but one constant endures: Madisonians want to be informed and they have a ravenous appetite for the printed word.

The number of newspapers and periodicals available in a city of just over 170,000 people is remarkable. Madison supports two daily newspapers, the morning *Wisconsin State Journal* (1988 circulation approximately 80,000) and the afternoon *Capital Times* (1988 circulation approximately 28,000), as well as an alternative weekly and a slick city monthly. In addition, two daily news-

Media: The Big Two

Madisonians have long been recognized as people who keep up with the world around them, an attitude reflected by their appetite for information. Madison may well support more newspapers, periodicals, and radio and television stations than any comparably sized city in the country.

Two of the most powerful, and interesting, of the Madison media are the daily newspapers—jointly owned under the name Madison Newspapers, Inc.—and the cable television company, TCI Cablevision of Wisconsin. Both have unusual histories and have at times been controverisal in Madison.

Madison has long had two daily newspapers: the *Capital Times*, which over the years has had a liberal editorial philosophy, clashing frequently with U.S. Senator Joseph McCarthy in the 1950s; and the *Wisconsin State Journal*, a more conservative newspaper.

For many years the *Wisconsin State Journal* was owned by Lee Enterprises, a media conglomorate based in Davenport, Iowa, while the *Capital Times* was owned locally by the Capital Times Company. That situation was thought to still be in place when, to the surprise of most Madisonians, it was revealed in 1986 that in fact the two newspapers had long ago consolidated into one company, Madison Newspapers, Inc. (MNI).

It came about in this manner: In 1934, the *State Journal* and the *Capital Times* entered into an informal agreement to sell advertising at a combination rate with profits split 50-50.

Fourteen years later, in 1948, they made it official, forming Madison Newspapers, Incorporated, to handle advertising and production services for both newspapers. At the time, both papers were delivered in the afternoon. The *State Journal* agreed to go morning, which at the time was viewed as a concession, and so they were given the right to publish a Sunday edition.

At the time, it was widely assumed, even among employees of the newspapers, that the papers had retained separate ownership and formed what in the newspaper business came to be known as a joint operating agreement, or JOA.

JOAs were officially legalized in 1970, when Congress passed the Newspaper Preservation Act. The idea behind the act was to preserve newspapers which would otherwise fail, and consequently a crucial component of any JOA was that the newspapers remain completely separate editorially.

In 1986, perhaps because they *did* want to merge some editorial functions of the *State Journal* and the *Capital Times* (primarily the two papers' libraries), MNI asked the U.S. Justice Department's Anti-Trust Division to investigate the old 1948 agreement and see what, in fact, had truly been formed.

On August 8, 1986, Justice Department attorney Fred Haynes wrote a letter to MNI's Washington lawyers which stated that the investigation had determined that the *State Journal* and the *Capital Times* had never been a JOA.

Instead, Haynes wrote, "after carefully examining this matter, we have concluded that the consolidation in 1948 . . . resulted in one entity, Madison Newspapers, Inc., owning both newspapers." In a 1987 interview with *Madison Magazine*, Haynes elaborated, "Basically we concluded that what took place in 1948 was a merger."

The situation as it now stands, then, has MNI owning both newspapers, while MNI is owned 50-50 by the *State Journal* and the *Capital Times*. MNI contracts with Lee Enterprises and the Capital Times Company to provide editorial content for the two papers. Needless to say, it's a complicated situation.

As of 1989, what some Madisonians feared—that the two papers would now merge editorially, and the city would lose a competing editorial voice—hadn't really happened.

The two papers did merge their libraries. A *Capital Times* editor now writes a regular weekly column in the Sunday *State Journal*. While many old-timers see this as a bad sign if not outright blasphemy, the two papers remain intensely competitive in most editorial areas. The pressure to beat one another on a story still exists, which gives life to daily journalism in the city.

The morning *State Journal* has steadily gained circulation over the years while the evening *Capital Times*, like afternoon papers almost

papers are published on the UW campus.

If that wasn't enough, nearly 2,000 Madisonians subscribe to the *New York Times* every day; that figure jumps to 3,000 on Sundays. Madison is also home to *The Progressive* magazine, a muckraking periodical of national repute, which in 1979 made headlines by publishing a guide to building an atomic bomb.

Madison has 17 ratio stations—11 FM and six AM. The city also has five full-power television stations: local affiliates of the three major commercial networks, an independent station, and a public broadcasting station licensed to the university. In 1987 a low-power station also began televising in Madison, with an emphasis on UW sports.

A major development for local television broadcasters occurred in 1988 when Madison was raised to the 90th-largest television market in the country, having previously been ranked 106th. The change came about with the inclusion of the Janesville region in Madison's area of dominant influence, an industry term of relevance to advertisers. Madison's jump into the top 100 is significant because many national advertisers buy only the top 100 markets.

Madison's appetite for information translates into a keen interest in local politics and government. The city of Madison operates under a mayoral/aldermanic form of government. Every two years, city residents elect a mayor and alderpersons representing 22 districts. In addition, Dane County residents elect a county executive and 41 district supervisors.

The races are often hotly contested, evidence that to govern in Madison and Dane County is a challenging and rewarding experience. That is even more the case now that Madisonians are working together toward common goals like never before.

FACING PAGE: Dramatic clouds gather in the late-afternoon sky over Lake Monona. Photo by Bruce Fritz

everywhere, has seen its circulation figures fall dramatically. Nevertheless, because they split the profits, both papers are economically sound.

If one of the criticisms of MNI has been their quasi- "monopoly" on Madison's daily newspaper business, the same complaint is sometimes raised about TCI Cablevision of Wisconsin, Madison's cable television company.

The company is owned by Denver-based Tele-Communications, Inc., (TCI), the largest operator of cable systems in the world. TCI had been a minority owner in Madison's cable company (then called Complete Channel TV) since 1971; in 1984, they bought it outright.

The 1984 Cable Communication Policy Act, passed by Congress, was a boon to the cable industry, and this applied to TCI in general and their Madison operation in particular.

A November 1986 *Madison Magazine* article revealed that in 1985 TCI had assets of $1.75 billion and reported 1985 revenues of $577 million. The same article noted that in Madison and its surrounding communities in 1986, TCI had more than 60,000 subscribers. On average, cable systems sell for around $1,400 a subscriber (before the 1984 Act, that figure was $800). Using the industry average, the Madison cable system in 1986 was worth $84 million.

TCI has an exclusive contract to be Madison's only cable franchisee until 1996. In return, the City of Madison gets a "franchise fee" —a percentage of gross revenues (5 percent in 1990).

Both city and cable company officials profess happiness with the agreement, which was signed in April 1983. The city gets a tidy sum in franchise fees and TCI Cablevision of Wisconsin gets exclusivity until 1996, plus the right to raise its rates without city approval beginning in 1989.

Some residents feel the rates are too high and the service too slow, but that is true nationwide and in any case, cable is not a public utility, and no one is forced to subscribe. As city-cable company relationships go, Madison's is actually one of the best.

CHAPTER FIVE

The Finer Things

T he cultural life in Madison can't be isolated from the city as a whole. The arts flourish in Madison—the city has been called "the Athens of the Midwest"—in large part because a commitment to and appreciation of culture is an integral part of the lives of many Madisonians, and, by extension, of Madison itself.

It's not articulated all that often. It's just expected that anyone who has chosen to live in such an aesthetically pleasing city, one so politically active, boasting one of the best universities in the world, would naturally hold an important place in his or her life for the arts.

Call it an attitude, a quiet sophistication. It's what the *New York Times* picked up on when Donna Shalala, a New Yorker, was selected as the UW-Madison's first woman chancellor in 1987. Writing of Madison, the *Times* likened it to New York: "It is a place of political, academic and cultural sophistication, with a cornucopia of performing

This performance of *Romeo and Juliet* in Spring Green was produced by the American Players Theatre, which provides perhaps America's best showcase of Shakespeare. Photo by Bruce Fritz

arts and progressive political tradition."

Most Madisonians probably enjoy comparisons to Athens more than to New York City, but the point is well taken. The city does offer an abundance of theaters, galleries, museums, music clubs, and more, a cultural feast certain to sate the appetite of even the most dedicated art aficionado.

To be sure, Madison has many of them. James Watrous, an emeritus professor of art history, author and founder of the Elvehjem Museum of Art (pronounced "LVM," it houses the collections of the University of Wisconsin), told *Madison Magazine* in 1987, "A greater percentage of people who live in this community are more attuned to—actually enjoy the arts—than would be the case in any other city I know of."

For many years Madison's cultural pulse could be taken almost exclusively at the University of Wisconsin. It was the UW which could draw world-class talents to Madison. Henry Fonda acted in *Mr. Roberts* at the Wisconsin Union Theater in the 1950s, and Alfred Lunt and Lynn Fontanne were booked there no less than five times from 1939 to 1949. In fact, Lunt and Fontanne starred in the Union Theater's premiere production, *The Taming*

of the Shrew, in 1939.

Today, while the UW is still a major fixture on the city's cultural landscape, there are other major players. In 1980 the American Players Theatre opened in Spring Green, Wisconsin, a short drive west of Madison. APT, as it is called, is an outdoor theater located on 71 wooded acres. Billed as America's only professional, classical theater center, APT has received a great deal of national press and acclaim. Devoted exclusively to classics, primarily Shakespeare, the theater features nationally experienced actors and directors.

In 1986 the Festival of the Lakes debuted in Madison under the direction of Edward Villela, the famed artistic director of the Miami City Ballet. The festival has become known as the week when "a city becomes a stage," and it is a truly extraordinary five-day spectacle of music, dance, stage, and visual imagery. The 1988 festival featured 850 performing and visual artists, 125 events, 25 premieres, world-class fireworks, a performance by the renowned Miami City Ballet, and a comprehensive exhibition of the life and work of Frank Lloyd Wright, the brilliant, mercurial architect who called Spring Green home.

Wright, incidentally, played a peripheral role in another major development on the Madison arts scene.

On October 14, 1941, speaking at the Union Theater, Wright introduced a plan for an auditorium-civic center for Madison—a facility, it was generally agreed, the city sorely needed.

Wright's plan, predictably, was daring and original. It called for the auditorium to be built on the Lake Monona Terrace at Law Park, with much of the building actually extending out over Lake Monona. Wright concluded, "The hope of actually creating the proposed Civic Center lies with youthful minded persons and with the common people."

Well, any youthful people who listened to Wright's speech that day were no longer young when Madison at long last got a civic center. It was 39 years after Wright's speech and it was located not on the Lake Monona Terrace but on State Street. Nevertheless, the

Madison Civic Center, which opened its doors in 1980, gave the city a centrally located home for a variety of local arts groups, as well as a facility that could handle major touring productions and stars.

Toward that end the Civic Center has done rather well. In 1987 alone, 350,000 people attended it to see shows like *Cats* and legendary performers including Mikhail Baryshnikov and Rudolf Nureyev. It may have taken a while, but once built, the Civic Center hit the ground running.

In any historical sense, of course, it was the university that carried the cultural ball in Madison. The Festival of the Lakes, American Players Theatre, and the Civic Center all came along in the 1980s.

One of the earliest theaters, and one which endures successfully today, is the Wisconsin Union Theater. Located in the Memorial Union on Langdon Street, the Union Theater is a 1,300-seat multipurpose performing arts facility serving students, faculty, Union members, and the community at large.

The Union Theater opened in 1939 and almost immediately had an effect on the national arts scene. This came about when Belgium's Pro Arte Quartet came to Madison in 1940 to perform. At the time, the Nazi occupation was making the thought of returning home very uncomfortable for the quartet, and the UW found a way to keep the group in Madison by developing a program called "artists in residence." (A half-century later the Pro Arte Quartet is still in Madison as artists in residence.)

Fan Taylor, the original publicity director of the Union Theater and overall director of the theater from 1945 to 1966, was selected as the first music program director for the Washington, D.C.-based National Endowment for the Arts in 1966. Upon arriving in Washington she instituted the artists in residence idea.

At UW-Madison other artists in residence over the years have included pianist Gunnar Johansen and still life painter Aaron Bohrod. Bohrod came in 1948. By 1987, in his 80th year, he continued to live in Madison. The city has a way of making people not want to leave.

The same year the Union Theater opened, 1939, art history professor James Watrous was trying to find a particular piece of art in the university collection, which was rather untidily stored beneath the UW administrative offices in a dark basement of Bascom Hall. So dismayed was Watrous by the arrangement that he spent the next 30 years fighting for a real museum. In 1970 he got it, when the Elvehjem Museum of Art, located at 800 University Avenue, opened.

The Elvehjem has since been recognized as one of the finest art museums in the country. Housing the collections of the University of Wisconsin, included in the museum's collections are over 14,000 works, ranging in date from 2,300 B.C. to the present. The collection includes significant holdings in

A juggler performs downtown. Photo by Bruce Fritz

European and American paintings, sculpture, prints, drawings, and decorative arts from the fifteenth to twentieth centuries.

The Elvehjem has also acquired a number of special collections, including Indian miniatures, Japanese prints, and European medals. One of the most interesting is the Joseph E. Davies collection of some 90 Russian and Soviet paintings, donated by Davies, the United States' second ambassador to the Soviet Union and a UW alumnus.

The presence of UW, then, provided Madison with a solid cultural diet, and the various theaters, musical programs, and museums helped whet the public's appetite for the arts. Small theater groups and galleries began opening around the city, and there was more talk about the need for a civic center. People in Madison were clearly excited about the arts.

The Union Theater's Fan Taylor witnessed the evolution firsthand, and she told *Madison Magazine* in 1987: "The population that wanted to take part in cultural programs could be adequately housed at the Union Theater when we opened it. As the years have gone by with the increased population, it's been necessary to find alternate spaces. This is all part of the reason why the city of Madison found it necessary to find its own space." As someone who had dedicated her life to the arts in Madison, Taylor was thrilled by this development. "I felt encouraged and flattered," she said, "that so many people had gone through training at the university and were now willing to branch out on their own in the arts. We always took the position that audiences breed audiences."

It can also be said that the growth of the arts in Madison has been on financially sound footing, effectively shattering the myth of arts organizations as beggars holding out a collective tin cup. For if as Taylor says audiences breed audiences, the arts in Madison also breed dollars, a fact that too often goes unrecognized by critics who frown upon, say, the Civic Center receiving a subsidy from the city. The truth is, never mind the arguments about what the arts do for the quality of life in Madison; they also generate a lot of dollars for themselves as well as ancillary dollars for other city businesses. Ralph Sandler, director of the Madison Civic Center since December 1981, says, "The arts have a serious economic impact on Madison. On a national average, for every one dollar spent on a ticket to an exhibit or concert, two and a half dollars are spent on something ancillary, services like taxis, parking, lodging and food."

In 1984 the Madison Art Center, a private, non-profit museum of modern and contemporary art located in the Civic Center, hosted a showing of 33 paintings by the world-renowned artist Georgia O'Keeffe, who grew up in the Madison area. The exhibition ran for six weeks and brought in $60,000 in admissions.

Of possibly greater import was a survey on the economic impact of the arts taken by the Art Center in association with the O'Keeffe exhibit. The Art Center's survey revealed that of people attending the O'Keeffe exhibition, 9,500 stayed overnight in the city. Halving that figure (two people per room) and multiplying by a (conservative) $40 per night average hotel room charge, the figures show that O'Keeffe visitors spent almost a half-million dollars *outside* the Art Center—more than seven times what was spent on admissions—and the survey didn't even measure what was spent in local retail shops and stores.

The recognition of the arts as an economic force in Madison is important because uninformed critics continue to harp at any public spending on the arts. It was that naysaying attitude, fortunately now a distinct minority view in Dane County, that kept the Civic Center from being built until 1980.

Way back in 1856 Jairus Fairchild, the first mayor of Madison, is on the record as having said, "What this city needs is an auditorium." Fairchild did indeed build a small auditorium on the second floor of city hall, but it was knocked out by a later administration that needed office space.

In 1910 landscape architect John Nolen was the first to suggest the shore of Lake Monona as a potential site for Law Park. Others, including Frank Lloyd Wright, agreed, with Wright going so far as to draw up plans.

Wright, who was born with a hefty chip on his shoulder, finally concluded grumpily that "there isn't enough civic spirit in Madison to do something great."

Wright was wrong—but it took a while. In 1954 a referendum passed allocating a $5.5-million bond issue for the Law Park site. It was on the verge of happening, but an anti-Wright faction kept placing stumbling blocks in the way until 1961. In that year, Henry Reynolds was elected mayor on a platform of abandoning the Monona terrace site.

It seemed Madison might never get the crown jewel its burgeoning arts community—and arts patrons—deserved. But in 1974 the city—under a young, activist, and controversial mayor named Paul Soglin—purchased the Capitol Theater, on State Street off the Capitol Square, with a plan to renovate it as Madison's first genuine, top-of-the-line auditorium complex.

On February 22, 1980, with Joan Mondale, wife of the former vice president, in attendance, the Civic Center opened with a performance by the Madison Symphony Orchestra. It had taken 124 years, but Mayor Fairchild's city at long last had a first-class auditorium. City residents were appreciative. In its first year the Civic Center took in $1.5 million in box office receipts.

The Civic Center today provides 110,000 square feet for the performing and visual arts, including the 2,200-seat Oscar Mayer Theatre, which hosts events such as Broadway plays (*Cats, Annie, Amadeus,* and *Broadway Bound*) among many others over the years); opera (*La Traviata* and *The Barber of Seville,* both by the New York City Opera National Company, in recent years); pop bands (although the big-name pop stars play the 9,000-seat Dane County Memorial Coliseum); and classical ballet, which reached undreamable heights in 1987 when both Baryshnikov and Nureyev danced in the Oscar Mayer Theatre.

Also included in the Civic Center complex is the Isthmus Playhouse, a 330-seat thrust stage theater, the Madison Art Center, the Madison Repertory Theatre, and Children's Theatre of Madison. In addition, the Civic Center features four meeting areas which can accommodate groups of 25 to 2,000.

Director Ralph Sandler is especially proud of the financial stability the center has attained, particularly in recent years, as well as the fact that the center hosts a number of free events for the community, including Concerts in the Crossroads on Thursdays and Saturdays, September through May.

As a reward for all the hard work, the Civic Center in 1987 received national recognition as one of the country's leading arts presenting institutions through a prestigious Challenge Grant of $200,000 from the National Endowment for the Arts. In 1988, the Civic Center was selected, with 20 other organizations, to be featured in a book profiling the most outstanding arts presenting organizations in the United States.

The Civic Center today is Madison's arts magnet and crown jewel, and if anything, its success has buoyed other arts organizations in the city. The Madison Art Center, where the Georgia O'Keeffe exhibition was held, continues to grow and expand its vision.

It moved into the Civic Center when that building opened in 1980; in its first year there, the Art Center's attendance grew from 25,000 to 100,000. A fund-raising drive in the early 1980s netted $130,000, and that and other money was used to improve the Art Center's physical quarters, to expand the staff, and to bring in more wide-ranging exhibits.

The changes were a success. The Art Center's budget by 1984 had doubled to $660,000 (with $35,000 in surplus for 1984). The center continues to conduct the successful Art Fair on the Square, and in 1988 it initiated a popular series called "Summer Music: Four Sunday Afternoons of Music by Wisconsin Composers," the first of which featured new music from nine composers.

Perhaps the Madison Art Center's greatest achievement has been establishing itself nationally (in 1985 it was accredited by the American Association of Museums, which called the center's exhibitions and programs "as good as any in the country") while at the same time showcasing the best talent locally.

Live theater also thrives in Madison. The American Players Theatre (APT) in nearby Spring Green battled financial setbacks throughout the 1980s but now appears to be on solid footing. Both private citizens and the government rallied to its support, and precisely because of this unprecedented outpouring of contributions, what may be America's best showcase of Shakespeare plays survives.

In a given season (June to October), APT will do a half-dozen or so different plays, most of which will be Shakespeare, drawing talent from all over the country.

One year the man who taught Errol Flynn how to fence for the movie *Captain Blood* came to APT to help stage an authentic Shakespearean sword battle. APT's first non-Shakespeare production, Christopher Marlowe's *Tamburlaine the Great,* debuted in 1983, and the troupe now regularly stages the works of other playwrights, notably Anton Chekhov.

There are many other successful theater troupes in Madison. The best-known and most professional is likely the Madison Repertory Theatre, a resident company of the Civic Center, which celebrated its 20th anniversary in 1988 with a typically diverse repertoire of plays, classic and original, often with a Midwest author or setting.

Other local theater in Madison includes the Madison Theatre Guild, one of the city's oldest arts institutions, which not only provides live entertainment for Madison—it encourages Madisonians to gain theater experience through volunteering. The Theatre Guild is affiliated with the Madison School District and produces five shows annually, September through June.

The ARK Repertory Theatre produces original and classical works of the avant-garde. Children's Theatre of Madison, a resident company of the civic center, produces plays for the entire family; it celebrated its 25th anniversary in 1989. One of the nation's best known "experimental" theater groups, Broom Street Theater, began in Madison in 1969, under the irreverent direction of Joel Gersmann, and two decades later both Gersmann and Broom Street are still going strong.

As can be witnessed by the 100,000 people annually who take in the Wisconsin Chamber Orchestra's (WCO) "Concerts on the Square," Madisonians also have a deep appreciation of music. Under the direction of David Crosby since 1970, the 28-member WCO features, along with their Square performances, an outstanding subscription series of concerts ranging from the Baroque to the contemporary.

The Madison Symphony Orchestra and Chorus plays nine concerts each season at the Civic Center. Distinguished guest artists and usually a pop concert or two add spice to the schedule.

Jazz has enjoyed something of a renaissance in Madison in recent years. Nationally known jazz artists such as Ben Sidran and Richard Davis have long called Madison home, but for a time they seemed to command more respect outside the city than they did in their own backyard.

The Madison Art Fair
on the square is always
a large draw. Photo
by Brent Nicastro

Live theater and music performance thrives in Madison, as in this Concert on the Square. Photo by Brent Nicastro

That has changed. In August 1987 the Friends of the Madison Civic Center and the Festival of the Lakes presented a two-day Jazzfest that brought people by the thousands to the downtown to hear jazz outdoors all day, and then "name" entertainment—Sidran and friends—at the Oscar Mayer Theatre in the Civic Center at night.

The following year, in October 1988, the same two organizations, along with Madison's weekly newspaper, *Isthmus,* held the two-day Isthmus Jazz Festival. The festival featured a series of workshops and informal performances in the Civic Center, a master class on jazz history by Richard Davis, and concerts by local jazz groups. The highlight of what many believe will become a significant annual jazz festival with a national reputation came the second night when the internationally renowned jazz musician Miles Davis performed in the Oscar Mayer Theatre. In 1989, the Jazz Festival was also a success, headlined by Ray Charles.

Madison is also rich in galleries and museums. Along with the Art Center and the Elvehjem, a number of smaller commercial galleries—including the Broden Gallery, Valperine Gallery, Grace Chosy Gallery, Fanny Garver Gallery, and several others, most either on or right off State Street—have become popular in recent years.

To fully appreciate Madison and Wisconsin culture, both residents and visitors to the city should find their way to the State Historical Society of Wisconsin, located on the campus end of State Street, eight blocks from the Square, and the State Historical Museum, at the other end, on the square on Carroll Street.

The Historical Society building, constructed in 1900, houses the historical library and state archives. Among its noteworthy holdings is a newspaper collection second in size only to that of the Library of Congress.

The State Historical Museum contains permanent exhibitions on Wisconsin Indians from prehistoric times to the present; they're located on the second floor. The first floor features a gift shop, orientation theater, and changing exhibitions. Further expansion and more exhibits are planned for floors three and four of the building, which originally housed a department store.

The Historic Preservation Office of the State Historical Society can provide direction to Madison buildings designed by one of the century's great architects, Frank Lloyd Wright, who lived in Madison from age 13

A local amusement center features state-of-the-art, high-tech thrill rides. Photo by Bruce Fritz

to 20 and who returned frequently to the city. Eight Madison buildings were designed by Wright, who nevertheless—as his inability to get his auditorium idea off the ground makes clear—was not wholly beloved in Madison.

Of the eight buildings, seven were private residences (though only six remain, as one was relocated in its entirety to Beaver Dam, Wisconsin). The eighth, the Unitarian Church on University Bay Drive, was completed in 1951 and featured a "praying hands" roof framing which offered a dramatic spectacle against the sky.

Wright *was* controversial. Though approved by referendum, his auditorium on the lake was never built. There were whispers of immorality in his private life, and further murmurings that he was a communist. Of the Monona Terrace design, Wright in one of his mellower moments said, "This dream was begun many years ago by a Madison boy who wondered why the city and the lakes never got together."

It may seem slightly ironic that today in Madison, Wright is revered. But it isn't, not really. Madison has grown in the last 50 years and so have people's acceptance of things different and daring.

A first-class civic center was built, if not on the lake, then on one of the most unique streets in the Midwest. And in Madison today a man like Wright is understood and apppreciated, while culture, and the arts as a whole, flourish.

Not all the diversions in and around Madison are man-made. Here, unique cloud formations gather in the area's skies. Photo by Bruce Fritz

CHAPTER SIX

The Sporting Life

T he year was 1978, and the University of Wisconsin hockey team had just returned from the NCAA Final Four Championship held that year in Providence, Rhode Island.

Wisconsin has won four national collegiate ice hockey championships, but 1978 was not the Badgers' year and they finished fourth. Nevertheless, something remarkable happened in Providence, something that spoke volumes about the spirit of Madison and what athletics mean to the city.

Several thousand Madisonians had followed the Badgers to Providence, and though the team lost, the Badger fans so delighted the host city with their enthusiasm, good will, and conviviality that the Providence Chamber of Commerce sent a representative to Madison with a plaque which read: "World's Greatest Hockey Fans."

It's not just hockey. On autumn Saturdays, fans pack Camp Randall Stadium to watch UW football. For years the UW ranked in the top 10 in national college football attendance despite rarely winning anything but the hearts of their fans.

In 1982 a professional minor league baseball team was established in Madison,

A snorkeler explores the remnants of a melted glacier at Devil's Lake. Photo by Bruce Fritz

and what happened? Fans poured in, the games became a "happening" (people dressed in fish costumes in honor of the Madison Muskies), and the phenomenon was written up in national publications.

What's Madison's secret? Probably that any event bringing together thousands of Madisonians is bound to transcend any mere game and become a rite of celebration. People who don't know a football from a hockey puck have been known to have fun at sporting events in Madison.

Maybe it shouldn't be surprising, then, to learn that one thing Madisonians enjoy as much as watching sports is participating in them. The city's 18,000 acres of lake surface are a haven for fishermen, swimmers, boaters, and water-skiers.

More than 6,000 men and women participate in the city summer softball program, and Madison's school-community Recreation Department also offers programs for all ages and abilities in sports such as basketball, soccer, hockey, and volleyball. Golf courses and bike paths abound. The opportunities to participate in sports in Madison year-round are endless.

There is also ample opportunity to simply appreciate nature and the outdoors. The author who in 1834 remarked on Madison's beautiful natural setting—a sentiment echoed in 1948 by *Life* magazine—wouldn't have to change a word today. Along with lakes, the city boasts 150 parks, a world-class zoo and the Arboretum, a 1,200-acre ecological laboratory of natural forests, prairie, and orchards located within the city and managed by the University of Wisconsin.

No question, the UW serves as centerpiece for the sporting and recreational life in Madison. The UW is a member of the Big Ten athletic conference and fields teams in 25 men's and women's sports.

Of all the teams fielded by the UW, it is the men's football team which elicits the most attention and emotion.

The Badgers have never won a Rose Bowl, the granddaddy of the New Year's Day bowl games to which the Big Ten champion is invited every year. Nevertheless, the UW was involved in what most observers regard as the best, most exciting Rose Bowl of all time, and though they lost, the Badgers' never-say-die spirit brought glory on themselves and a pride to the city which endures to this day.

It was the 1963 Rose Bowl, and Wisconsin was playing the number one ranked University of Southern California. The Badgers had also played in the 1960 Rose Bowl and had been humiliated, 44-8, by the University of Washington.

In 1963 it appeared it would be the same old story. With only 12 minutes left in the game, Wisconsin trailed USC 42-12, and to make matters worse, a fog the Rose Bowl lights couldn't handle had rolled in and the game would be finished in near darkness.

But in the gathering dusk a remarkable thing happened. Wisconsin staged a dramatic comeback, cutting the lead to 42-37 with just over a minute to go, and indeed almost won by nearly blocking a punt on the game's final play. It was a tremendous game, a fact borne out by the authors of *The Book of Lists,* who chose it as one of the six most dramatic sporting events of all time.

That drama and spirit have remained with UW football, although, alas, there have been more losing seasons than winners. No matter. Badger fans are loyal, and win or lose they have fun. Thousands tailgate before and after the games. They make a day of it.

It's something visiting coaches and players have remarked on over the years. Given the enthusiasm level at Camp Randall Stadium, one would think the fans were cheering a team that routinely won national championships. It's partly explained by the superb UW Marching Band, under the longtime direction of Michael Leckrone. Leckrone, a born showman and a man of great energy and personality, keeps the fans fired up all the way to the famed "fifth quarter," when

at game's end everyone is invited down onto the field to dance and party with the band.

That kind of infectious enthusiasm was embodied by Elroy Hirsch, the former pro football star who served as director of UW athletics from 1969 to 1986. Hirsch had played football at UW and then gone on to star in the pros and become an executive with the Los Angeles Rams. In 1969 Hirsch returned home to Wisconsin and to an athletic department that was $200,000 in debt, not counting a decade of deferred maintenance. Hirsch revitalized UW athletics, got it back on sound financial footing, and when he retired thousands of his friends threw an emotion-filled party for him at the UW Fieldhouse.

Hirsch's retirement and the sudden heart attack death, in 1986, of football coach Dave McClain (who led the Badgers to two bowl games), slowed UW athletics for a time. The football team struggled in the late '80s and attendance declined. In late 1989, however, the UW administration, led by Chancellor Donna Shalala, restated their commitment to the football program, and promised to do whatever is necessary to get both Badger football and the athletic department moving forward again.

One program that didn't need revitalizing, which has in fact prospered for two decades, is ice hockey. Badger hockey is a phenomenon akin to Indiana basketball or Oklahoma football, a blend of great performance by the team and the most intense fan loyalty. Since 1968, UW hockey games have been played at the plush Dane County Memorial Coliseum. From the early 1970s on, the Friday and Saturday night games have been sellouts, with 8,600 fans, tops in the nation, packing the Coliseum to cheer the Badgers and revel in the raucous atmosphere.

The redoubtable Mike Leckrone and his band are also present at the hockey games. It was at a hockey game that the band first played the "Budweiser" song, now an institution at UW sports events, with a change in the chorus which concludes: "When you say Wis-con-sin, you've said it all."

If there was a gap for the sports spectator in Madison, it came in the summers—at least until 1982. That year, the Madison Muskies debuted, playing 72 home games at Warner Park on Madison's East Side. The Muskies are a Class A farm team of the Oakland A's.

While everyone was excited about bringing professional baseball to Madison, not even the wildest

ABOVE AND FAC-
ING PAGE: The
Badgers have never
won a Rose Bowl,
that granddaddy of
the New Year's Day
bowl games to which
the Big Ten champion
is invited every year.
But the team's never-
say-die spirit brings
glory on themselves
and their community.
Photos by Bruce Fritz

optimists could have dreamed how the city would embrace the team. Once again, in the Madison tradition, Muskie games became an event. Madison led the Midwest League in attendance, and the Muskie fans really got into the game: wearing fish hats, clapping the "fish clap," throwing fish sticks, singing, chanting, and having a great time.

The novelty of the Muskies and the intensity of the fans may have diminished slightly over the years, but the games remain a popular way to spend a summer evening in Madison.

If the city now boasts spectator sports on a year-round basis, the same is even more true for participants.

As just one example: Madison is certifiably golf-crazy. There are an abundance of city-owned public courses as well as privately owned courses open to the public in the Madison area. Of several private golf courses, two are of particular note: Maple Bluff, on the far East Side, which in 1987 *Golf Digest* rated as the fourth-best golf course in Wisconsin, and Nakoma, on the near West Side, which was the home course for Andy North while he was learning the game.

North, who continues to make his home in Madison, thrilled the city with his dramatic, one-stroke victory in the 1978 United States Open Championship at Cherry Hills in Denver. With a strong wind hampering his concentration, North needed to make a four-foot putt on the tournament's last hole for his victory. He addressed it, backed away, and then calmly stepped up and stroked it in.

Some people say anyone can win a major golf championship once, and North, plagued by injuries to his knees and back, had some ups and downs after his Open victory. But then in 1985, at Detroit's Oakland

Hills course, North made a triumphant return by winning a *second* U.S. Open title, establishing himself as one of the game's greats.

Of the public courses in Madison, Yahara Hills, a 36-hole layout on the city's far southeast side, is popular because there is usually no waiting, an enviable circumstance at a time when the golfing boom has clogged the fairways in many cities. The city's most popular public course is probably still Odana Hills, 18 holes in the middle of a residential district on the city's West Side. Odana is well maintained despite the fact it gets a great deal of play; the addition of a fully automated watering system has helped immensely.

Odana is also a challenging course. Arnold Palmer and Gary Player played an exhibition at Odana in the 1960s, and Palmer, after birdieing the last hole to set a new course record, called it one of the finest public courses he'd seen.

Along with Yahara and Odana, the city operates two nine-hole courses, Glenway and Monona, and between them the courses are geographically distributed as to allow most Madison residents access within a 10-minute drive.

In addition, construction began in 1988 on a University of Wisconsin golf course, which will be open to the public and located just west of the city limits in the town of Verona. Designed by the

It is estimated that Madison has more bicycles than cars, and the city contains more than 100 miles of bike paths. Photos by Brent Nicastro

TOP: In May, bicycle races are held around the Capitol Square. Photo by Bruce Fritz

BOTTOM: Some 10,000 runners take part in the "Crazy Legs Run" each spring. Photo by Bruce Fritz

Increasingly, the city's bike trails are also teeming with runners and walkers. Madisonians have embraced the national health kick, and they're joining health clubs, working out, and staying aerobically fit in record numbers. Each spring, before the annual UW intrasquad football game, some 10,000 runners take part in the "Crazy Legs Run," a charitable event named in honor of the former UW athlete and athletic director, Elroy "Crazy Legs" Hirsch.

Tennis enjoyed a boom in Madison in the late 1970s, and if it has leveled off somewhat, the sport remains extremely popular. The city has dozens of outdoor public courts, many located in parks or at schools. In cold weather, tennis buffs may play indoors at the Nielsen Tennis Stadium, one of the largest indoor tennis facilities in the country (open to UW students and faculty), and at either of two private tennis clubs in the city, the John Powless Tennis Center on the West Side and the Cherokee Country Club for East Siders.

famed golf course architect Robert Trent Jones, Jr., it is expected to be one of the finest courses in the state of Wisconsin.

Madisonians who want to work out some golf course frustrations by taking a bike ride will find plenty of enjoyable routes in a city that has been called the "Bicycle Capital of the Midwest." It is estimated that Madison has more bicycles than cars and the city boasts nearly 100 miles of bike paths.

There are any number of scenic bike trips within the city, but two stand out: one circles Lake Monona, winding through several parks and gardens; and one runs along Lake Mendota on the UW campus, beginning near the Memorial Union and finishing at the tip of Picnic Point, a slender peninsula which juts into Lake Mendota at the far west end of the campus. Many people will want to park their bikes and hike around Picnic Point, one of the loveliest areas in the city. Its 120 acres are owned by the UW and feature unusual vegetation, granite bolders, and five Indian burial mounds dating back to the year A.D. 300.

Complete maps of the Madison bikeway system are available at local libraries as well as city hall; biking enthusiasts might also consider joining one of several local clubs dedicated to bicycle touring.

Fans of water sports are equally well served in Madison. Boaters have their pick of 40 launching sites in Dane County. Fishermen among them will find the Madison lakes justly famous for first-rate fishing for a variety of species: perch, crappie, bluegill, walleye, bass, and northern pike.

There are 13 beaches with lifeguards and bathhouses on Madison lakes, and a total of 92 miles of shoreland in Dane County. The lakes are also ideal for sailing and waterskiing, two of the most popular participant sports in the city.

The freezing of the lakes in the winter does not bother the sports-minded Madisonian. On the lakes and at more than 40 parks in Madison ice skating areas are available, many of them lighted and equipped with warming houses. Several also have hockey rinks.

The success of UW hockey over the years has

helped contribute to the growth of a strong junior hockey program in Madison. Likewise, the extraordinary success of Madison native Eric Heiden at the 1980 Olympics has boosted the popularity of speed skating.

Local residents could be forgiven for calling the 1980 Winter Games the "Madison Olympics." Not only did Eric Heiden capture an unprecedented five gold medals in speed skating, but his sister Beth was also a speed skating medalist, and two Madisonians, Bob Suter and Mark Johnson, earned gold medals playing on the U.S. hockey team which so dramatically upset the Soviets to win the gold medal.

Skiing—both downhill and cross-country—are also popular with Madisonians during the winter months. In the city itself there are several cross-country areas, with a total of over 100 miles of trails throughout Dane County. Within an hour's drive of the city are four downhill ski resorts.

Most of the cross-country areas inside the city are located in parks, something Madison has in abundance, with over 150 to choose from. One of the nicest, Vilas Park, a favorite for sports activities and picnics—and located on Lake Wingra—is adjacent to Madison's

Henry Vilas Zoo.

The zoo, which attracts over a half-million visitors annually, is widely recognized as one of the finest medium-sized zoos in the country. It is home to more than 1,000 animals of 350 species.

The Vilas Zoo is one of 13 zoos in North America to have attained accreditation from the American Association of Zoological Parks and Aquariums, and is one of 55 zoos in the United States to be approved by the United States Department of Agriculture to examine certain exotic specimens. The Vilas Zoo breeding program—specifically with orangutans, Siberian tigers, spectacle bears, penguins, and camels—is renowned worldwide.

The UW Arboretum, located within the city on the

The freezing of the lakes in the winter does not bother the sports-minded Madisonian. Photo by Brent Nicastro

The Henry Vilas Zoo attracts more than a half-million visitors annually. It is home to more than 1,000 animals of 350 species. Photos by Bruce Fritz

near West Side, is also of world-class distinction. Maintained by the UW for research and instruction, it is open to the public and is one of the finest and most popular places for Madisonians and their visitors to spend their leisure moments—hiking, biking, cross-country skiing or taking one of the free public nature tours offered on weekends. The Arboretum's 1,260 acres provide living examples of the major plant communities: prairies, woodlands, marshes, and ponds. There are also native trees, migratory game, and more than 200 varieties of lilacs.

A more controlled, but equally beautiful natural setting can be found on the other side of the city at the Olbrich Botanical Gardens, a 51.7-acre park open all year. Charging no admission fee, it offers a variety of horticultural displays including annuals, perennials, shrubs, hybrid roses, lilies, dahlias, and spring bulbs.

Of course, Madison and the surrounding area also provide man-made works of such beauty and skill as to be must-sees for locals and visitors alike. The Governor's Executive Residence, located on Lake Mendota in Maple Bluff, was built in 1928 and is an example of Classic Revival architecture. It's open most of the year for public tours.

Within a half-hour's drive of Madison is the Circus World Museum, near Baraboo, which boasts the largest collection of circus wagons in the world, along with a wild animal menagerie and big-top circus.

About the same distance from Madison is the House on the Rock, near Spring Green and the American Players Theatre. A truly awesome structure built atop a chimney of rock some 450 feet above Wyoming Valley, it contains many fascinating collections and exhibits.

Finally, one must note Madison's proximity (45 miles) to the legendary Wisconsin Dells, perhaps the Midwest's preeminent vacation area. The Dells offers a mix of great natural splendor—boat trips through the upper and lower Dells—and a variety of commercial entertainment, including water slides, Wild West shows, and a famed water ski show hosted by Tommy Bartlett.

For a city with so much going on in terms of business, government, and higher education, one of Madison's unique charms is that people here also know how to enjoy themselves. Having fun is not always as easy as it sounds, but clearly, Madisonians know how to work hard *and* play hard. It's a good mix and an important part of a vibrant city.

A crew team works
out on Lake Monona.
Photo by Bruce Fritz

Epilogue

Someone once said the past is prologue, and the phrase has rarely been more apt than for Madison as it enters the 1990s.

In 1989, city voters elected as mayor a man who led the city for six years during the 1970s, a man who, while at times controversial, has always had the ability to make things happen in Madison.

Paul Soglin will serve Madison as mayor until at least 1991. He has indicated a desire to seek reelection, and in '91 the mayor's term in Madison will be extended to four years.

His fingerprints are already all over the city. In the 1970s Soglin was the driving force behind many important developments in Madison, including the building of the Civic Center, the Lake Monona bike path, the State Street Mall, and the mass transit system.

Soglin's forceful personality, which caused some people to look askance in the past, has mellowed with age. In his new but familiar role as mayor leading Madison into the '90s (Soglin was out of public life for the decade 1979-1988), he has encouraged useful compromise without losing the edge that always seems to bring out the best in himself and others.

Much more than in the past, the business community in Madison is getting along with Soglin, and they respect him. The same can be said of Rick Phelps, the new Dane

A lone fisherman tries his luck on the shores of Lake Mendota. Photo by Brad Crooks

County executive who demonstrated both skill and savvy during his first months in office.

Soglin and Phelps are just two of a wide array of talented people who will help steer Madison toward the 21st century.

In a recent article titled "The Future of the City: 2000," *Madison Magazine* observed, "From James Doty to John Nolen to Frank Lloyd Wright, Madison has been a city of dreamers. And its modern-day dreamers have visions of a future more beautiful than the past, more dynamic than the present."

Worthy goals, to be certain. Is it possible Madison in the year 2000 will have a downtown convention center serving as a gateway to a three-tiered mall and park cascading to a marina on Lake Monona? That the local economy will be even more vibrant as Madison-based high-tech companies service the booming communications industry? That the much-heralded quality of life in the city will remain among the best in the country or even improve?

One might venture to say it's not only possible, but probable. Madisonians love their city too much to remain satisfied with a status quo. And the building blocks for advancement are in place.

"The university provides the strong scientific base you must have in an entrepreneurial community," UW engineering professor John Klus told *Madison Magazine*. "The connection between the university and the business community is already good, better than almost any place I've come across. And it will become stronger.

"In order for new business to thrive," Klus continued, "there's a real need for acceptance of diverse individuals. Wisconsin and the Midwest don't do that very well. But Madison is the one clear exception.

"That may make us attractive to all kinds of kooks, but it also provides a healthy climate for the entrepreneur, for the risk-taker."

How appropriate that Klus used the word "diverse." In the introduction to this book it was observed that Madison's great strength lies in its diversity. Big city sophisticated, small town friendly. Hard working, fun loving. Above all a vibrance, an abundant energy, a sense that all things are possible.

Madison's future is bright because the city—which is to say, its people—have never stopped trying to be better. A new century dawns? Madison is eager to meet it head-on.

PART TWO

Madison's Enterprises

Photo by Brent
Nicastro

CHAPTER SEVEN

Networks

M adison's energy, communications, and transportation firms keep power, information, and products circulating inside and outside the area.

Photo by Brent Nicastro

Wisconsin Power and Light Company

"We are preparing Wisconsin Power and Light Company to compete successfully in the new energy marketplace," says James R. Underkofler, chairman, president, and chief executive officer of WPL Holdings, Inc. The holding company is the parent firm of Wisconsin Power and Light Company, a 65-year-old investor-owned electric, gas, and water utility, which employs 2,700 people. WP&L's service territory encompasses 603 cities, villages, and towns across 16,000 square miles in central and southern Wisconsin. The energy marketplace of the 1990s will pose some new challenges, including the effects of deregulation and the ever-increasing costs of building plants to generate power.

But WP&L is well prepared to respond to new challenges, according to Erroll B. Davis, Jr., president and chief executive officer of the utility. "We have an excellent and creative work force, an outstanding safety record, and efficient and well-maintained generating stations that consistently have exceeded national and state averages," says Davis.

One key component of WP&L's plan for the future is economic development. "We've been committed to Wisconsin and its economy since the company began," says E. Dean Baumgardner, WP&L's economic development manager. "WP&L's strength as a company depends on the local community. No matter how good our decisions are as a company, we can't be successful if the local economy is not strong."

WP&L has traditionally concentrated on industrial recruitment, and this is still a key service. The firm offers a computer data base and aerial photography of industrial sites and buildings, a Site Flight helicopter service for prospects, as well as direct mail, print, telemarketing, and other promotional campaigns.

Industrial recruitment efforts emphasize the many business advantages to locating in Wisconsin. The strong work ethic means that Wisconsin's worker production is as much as 31 percent higher than the national average. Wisconsin's energy costs are already low, and WP&L offers the lowest industrial electric rates in the state—35 percent lower than neighboring Illinois.

WP&L has also broadened its economic development efforts into three other key areas: business retention, expansion, and development; community outreach; and public policy initiatives. WP&L's businesses retention programs help businesses that are already located in its service area. The company offers programs such as the Bright

ABOVE & BELOW: Wisconsin Power and Light Company is a 65-year-old investor-owned, electric, gas, and water utility that employs 2,700 people and serves 603 cities, villages, and towns across 16,000 square miles in central and southern Wisconsin.

Ideas for Business energy-efficiency service, infrared thermography for detecting electrical problems, and a power quality analysis that could help prevent equipment malfunctions.

WP&L's innovative selling to the government program, which began in 1986, has expanded into a procurement consortium whose mission is to assist Wisconsin businesses in competing for—and winning—state and federal government contracts. This joint effort involving resources from the state, university, and vocational colleges has resulted in more than $200 million in new government contracts for WP&L customers.

A top priority at WP&L is improving the economic strength of communities. WP&L's partnership with local communities includes operation of a Rural Development Training Center. The center provides seminars, training material, and other resources for the use of community leaders.

Wisconsin Power and Light Company is committed to making the difference in the quality of life of the communities it is privileged to serve.

WMSN Television

The master control room behind the scenes at WMSN Television.

"Channel 47 was one of the first TV stations in the United States to use the new Betacam half-inch videotape format exclusively," according to William Schereck, general manager of WMSN-TV, Channel 47. "And we were one of the very first TV stations in the country to install a robotic Betacart machine, which allows one master control operator to load and play programs and commercials alone." This is particularly important for the locally owned Fox Station affiliate, since it is all locally programmed except for two hours on Saturday and four hours on Sunday night. "Now the Betacart machine is the industry standard," Schereck says, "and we look like gurus."

Madison's newest TV station went on the air June 8, 1986, broadcasting from its new facility on the site of the old Big Sky Drive-In on Madison's far West Side. The station's 38 employees have access to 15 MacIntosh and 10 IBM computers. "We are probably the most computerized TV station in the United States," says Schereck. Computers are used for word processing, spreadsheets, graphics, and character (type) generation. An eight-track recording studio, complete with a Yamaha DX7 stereo synthesizer, makes it possible for station staff to compose custom music and sound effects. And an Aurora graphics system offers a computer "paintbox" for commercial and industrial production. Channel 47 has two Sony BVP30 cameras that can be used either for studio or field production, as well as a van for use in the field.

The 13,500-square-foot studio is as up to the minute as the equipment it contains. There are six separate heating and air-conditioning systems in the building, with 27 control zones to maintain maximum conditions for the equipment. The technical area has computer flooring and non-load-bearing walls so that the building can be modified without extensive construction work. A 3M routing switcher makes it possible to reconfigure equipment without rewiring. "This gives us tremendous flexibility in the utilization of our equipment," Schereck says.

Channel 47 sees its niche in the Madison area TV market as an alternative to the three major network affiliates. "We counterprogram," Schereck says. "If the three majors are running news programs, we run sitcoms. If they have soaps on, we run cartoons. And when they're running sitcoms, we run movies." In fact, because of all the cartoons Channel 47 broadcasts, "We own the kids' business

in this market," Schereck says.

Channel 47 also broadcasts a lot of sports, including the Milwaukee Brewers, the Milwaukee Bucks, and UW-Madison basketball and hockey games. "We are able to offer a lot more sports than the network affiliates because of their

WMSN offices and studios on Madison's West Side.

commitments to the networks," Schereck says. On the other hand, Channel 47 does not broadcast a daily news show.

Movies are an important part of Channel 47's lineup. At least one movie airs every weeknight, and several air on the weekends. (The movie that runs at midnight on Fridays is known as "Big Sky Theater," in honor of the drive-in theater that was a Madison landmark for many years and where generations of Madison teenagers,

including Schereck, learned their early social skills.)

Locally produced programming includes the "Jonathan Barry Show" (public affairs), the "Jeff Sauer Show" (sports), the "Tom Treblehorn Show" (sports), "Rural Route/Popcorn" (movies), and public service announcements such as promotions for the Madison Civic Center.

Channel 47's programming has been well received. Revenues increased 37 percent in 1988, "and the trend continues," Schereck says. Schereck does not feel that Channel 47's success has come at the expense of older, more established stations in the Madison market. "We're not just taking advertisers away from the other stations. We put 100 new advertisers on the air last year," he says.

In addition, "One of our strategic goals when we

The WMSN Television staff and board of directors.

signed on was to help capture Rock County for Madison," he adds—a goal that has now been accomplished. With the addition of Rock County to the Madison market's ADI (area of dominant influence, or broadcast coverage area), the Madison market moved from number 106 nationally to number 90 among media markets.

Channel 47 is owned by the Channel 47 Limited Partnership, which is made up of four general partners and 60 limited partners. The four general partners are Nathan Brand, Phyllis Lovrien, Fred Mohs, and Paula Pruett. Media Management Corporation, whose president is Steven Pruett, manages the station and was also in charge of building it.

"We are well on our way to being financially a success as well as a ratings success," Schereck says. "It's our intention to displace one of the network affiliates. We may always be fourth in ratings, but I don't believe we will always be fourth in revenues."

Shockley Communications Corporation

From concept to completion, Pro-Video has established a high standard for video production. Next door, you'll be toe tapping to 1950s, 1960s, and 1970s music with Madison's oldies station, 94.9FM WOLX. Located on Madison's near west side overlooking the UW-Madison Arboretum is the headquarters of Shockley Communications Corporation. This privately held company was formed in 1985 by Terry and Sandy Shockley. The firm operates ProVideo and WOLX-FM in Madison and KDAL-AM/96 Lite FM in Duluth/Superior, Minnesota. The company is positioned for growth and looks to future expansion in broadcast communications.

sin to offer all-component video production—video in its purest form," Shockley says. ProVideo produces TV commercials for both adver-

listeners hear up-to-the-minute news reports and professional weather from Weather Central, the Midwest's largest private weather-

WOLX-FM plays "oldies" throughout the day and night with up-to-the-minute news and weather reports.

ProVideo

ProVideo is a video and postproduction facility offering studio and location video production, as well as off-line editing, on-line editing, and duplicating services to commercial and industrial clients throughout the Midwest. "ProVideo is the only video production company in Wiscon-

tising agencies and direct accounts. The firm also produces industrial videos (for sales training, annual reports, and corporate presentations) for a wide variety of private companies and the public sector. Jerry Emmerich, ProVideo's general manager, designed its innovative eye-to-eye editing suite. The editing suite is inter-format, handling one-inch, Beta Cam, Beta Cam SP, and three-quarter-inch video tape with full color correction. Location and studio recording include high-end cameras and support gear.

WOLX-FM

Radio station 94.9FM WOLX sends a powerful radio signal throughout all of south-central Wisconsin. The station plays a 24-hour format featuring "all oldies all the time." Hourly,

Shockley Communications Corporation's Pro-Video is a video and postproduction facility offering studio and location video production and other video-related services to commercial and industrial clients throughout the Midwest.

forecasting center. The Shockleys emphasize community involvement, and the radio station is active in the Taste of Madison, the Dane County Fair, the Circus World Museum in Baraboo, and many charitable events.

Corporate president Terry Shockley has a longtime presence in the Madison media market, combining local service and industry leadership. His activities include serving as past president of the Greater Madison Chamber of Commerce, former chairman of the ABC-TV affiliate board of governors, and past president of the Wisconsin Broadcasters Association.

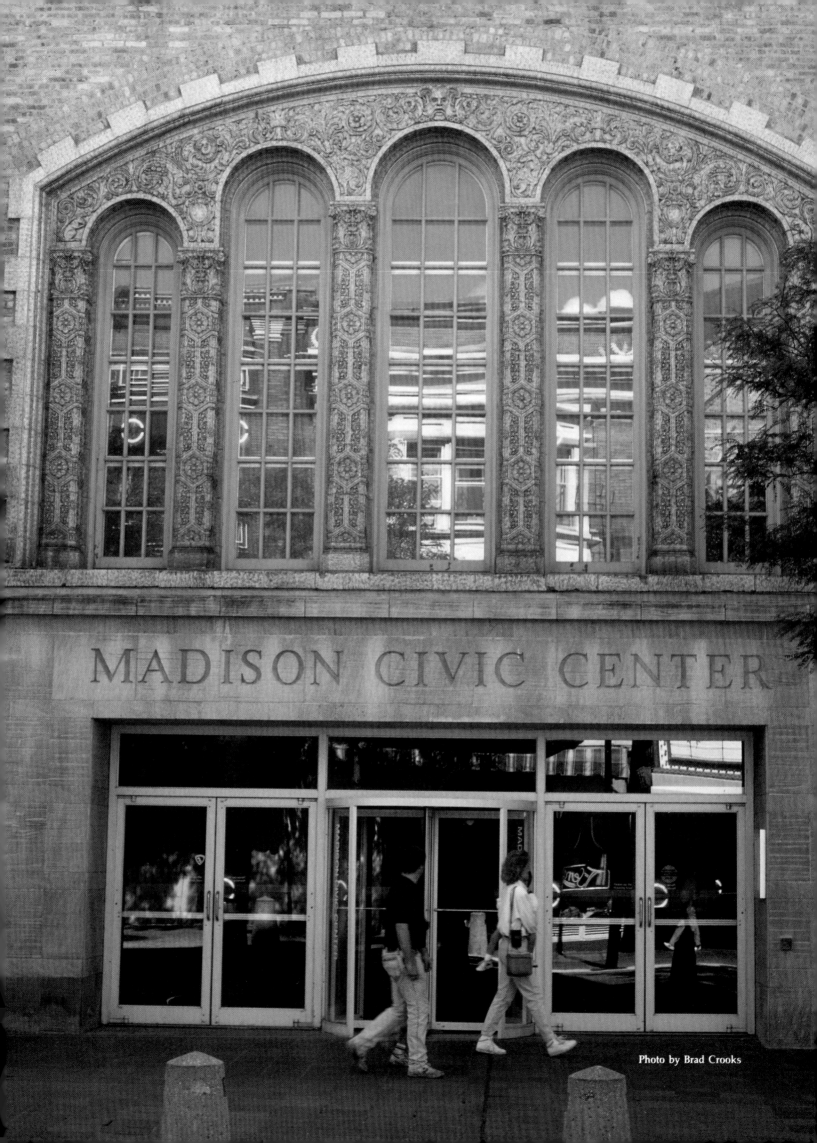

MADISON CIVIC CENTER

Photo by Brad Crooks

CHAPTER EIGHT

Manufacturing

P roducing goods for individuals and industry, manufacturing firms provide employment for many Madison-area residents.

Photo by Bruce Fritz

Graber Industries, Inc.

"Our products are found in stores ranging from Prange's in Madison to Harrod's in London," says James M. Sheridan, president of Graber Industries, Inc. "We are one of the fastest growing companies in our industry." Founded in 1939 to manufacture the Badger Crane drapery hanger, Graber Industries today manufactures a wide variety of custom and commercial window-covering products. Graber product

sold under both the Graber label and chain-store labels. All of the drapery hardware sold at Sear's Roebuck and Co. is manufactured by Graber; the firm has won a Sears Partners in Progress Award two years in a row. Graber also supplies most of the fabric used in the vertical blinds sold in JCPenney stores. Graber products are sold in many other decorating, specialty, and retail stores, as well as in

chitect for two years to make the blinds less expensive to install. "We are an industry leader in product development," Sheridan says.

Graber has been developing new products since it was founded. In 1939 John N. Graber helped his daughter, Marie, hang draperies around Venetian blinds. Graber invented and patented an adjustable drapery crane called the Badger Crane, which was the company's first product.

After John Graber died in 1966, the family sold the business to Consolidated Foods Corporation, who expanded the product line. Springs Industries, Inc., headquartered in Fort Mill, South Carolina, purchased Graber Industries in 1979.

Today Graber runs its production lines 24 hours per day, seven days per

Graber Industries' employees gather to salute the company's 50th anniversary.

lines include drapery hardware, window shades, horizontal blinds, vertical blinds, and pleated shades. They are available in a wide variety of contemporary colors, textures, shapes, and sizes.

Graber is well known for its consumer product lines, which are

home centers throughout the United States and in 27 foreign countries. In 1987 Graber received a U.S. "E" Flag Award for its success in the export business.

Though less visible to the general public, Graber's commercial sales division is also growing. The company won a recent contract to supply vertical blinds for a very vertical building—AT&T's new 60-story office building in Chicago. Graber worked with the building ar-

week. The company employs about 1,500 people, mostly at its 380,000-square-foot headquarters on Highway 12 in Middleton. The firm also has sales offices in New York City, Atlanta, Chicago, Dallas, and Los Angeles.

Sheridan attributes the success of Graber Industries, Inc., to its employees. "What sets us apart, he says, "is the caliber of the people we have. This is very much a can-do operation."

DRG Medical Packaging

The world leader in the manufacture of medical packaging has its U.S. headquarters in a 170,000-square-foot facility on Lien Road on Madison's east side. DRG produces medical packaging for products ranging from adhesive bandages to complex surgical procedure kits. "We have the broadest product range, the latest technology, and the largest dollar sales in our served market," says John R. Bath, general manager of Madison's operations. "During a short visit to the emergency room of any hospital anywhere in the United States, the doctors and nurses would almost certainly be using medical packaging made here in Madison."

DRG Medical Packaging specializes in the production of high-quality, sterilizable packaging materials. "In Madison alone we produce 20 million pounds per year of coated and printed papers and films for use by producers of medical supplies," states Bath. DRG uses all of the common medical packaging materials, including papers, flat and thermoformable films, laminates, and Tyvek®, to manufacture its products. The company uses flexographic printing processes as well as rotogravure for very demanding designs. Highly technical heat-seal or cold-seal coatings are applied by rotogravure, air knife, or flexographic methods.

Quality is a key to success in the medical packaging field, according to Jay L. Smith, president of the company. "We believe that quality must be built into a prod-

DRG Medical Packaging's corporate headquarters in Madison.

uct during each step in the manufacturing process," Smith says. "We have put into place a unique proprietary system called CQS— Complete Quality System."

There are extraordinary demands for quality control in the medical packaging field. "Every business ought to be striving for high quality, but in our business, we have an absolute responsibility to provide quality," Smith says. He adds that DRG's internal quality-assurance standards are so stringent that "many customers have now eliminated incoming quality-control testing on DRG shipments and rely instead on our letter of certification."

Accuracy and attention to detail are paramount. The printing on packaging material not only gives critical information pertaining to the device contained and its use, but it also provides the coded signals that fast-running packaging machines use to make perfect packages consistently. As Bath

points out, "An incorrect signal caused by inaccurate printing would produce a lot of bad packages very quickly!"

The firm's attention to quality has paid off in a compounded growth rate that has averaged 23 percent per year for 20 years. "In that time, DRG Medical Packaging has grown to the point where its sales are double those of its nearest competitor," states Bath. Such growth has relied both on DRG's attention to quality products and on its employees' productivity. "We have an excellent work force with very little turnover," he says. "Wisconsin workers have got a

very good work ethic, and that has really assisted us."

DRG manufactures sterilizable packaging materials, mostly in the form of rolls of paper and film, through which manufacturers of medical devices sterilize their products after the packaging process. Medical packaging thus involves more than simply converting various materials into packaging for medical products, Smith points out. "We are a supplier of specialized packaging to provide a sterile barrier against microbiological invasion. And in this highly technical industry, subject to rapidly changing material and equipment technology, it is essential to our survival and success that we are always abreast of new innovations

and opportunities," Smith says.

DRG's customers may specify a wide variety of properties in the medical packaging they order. Seal strength, porosity, and compatibility with one or more of the accepted sterilization methods can all vary, depending on the end use for the packaging. Each kind of medical packaging requires particular properties that must be designed and engineered into each of DRG's products. "We believe we can design medical packaging materials to meet the requirements of any medical device manufacturer," Bath says.

DRG Medical Packaging was founded by Robert W. Smith in 1958. Initially called the Fordem Company, it manufactured quality flexible packaging materials for the food industry. Jay and Jerry Smith, Robert's sons, joined the business in 1963. In the late 1960s the

Smiths set out to take Fordem out of commodity-related food packaging materials and into the market niche of medical packaging in a three-year time period. Within a decade Fordem was the leading U.S. manufacturer of medical packaging and had begun to expand into European markets.

In 1982 British-based DRG (the Dickinson Robinson Group), a company with 14,000 employees worldwide and sales of $1.5 billion, purchased Fordem from the Smith family and renamed it DRG Medical Packaging.

With the joining of the two companies, DRG became the world's largest supplier of medical packaging products. Manufacturing overseas in New Zealand, Australia, France, England, Ireland, and Puerto Rico, and domestically in Ashland, Massachusetts; Mount Holly, New Jersey; and, of course, in Madison, DRG Medical Packaging today dominates the worldwide medical packaging field. Says Smith, "Among our customers, we are fortunate to count virtually all of the top names among manufacturers of medical devices."

FROM LEFT TO RIGHT: Essential to the company's success is keeping abreast of innovations and opportunities in this highly technical industry.

Wisconsin employees' excellent work ethic is a major contributor to the company's success.

Accuracy and attention to detail are essential to meet the demands of today's high-speed packaging machinery.

The W.T. Rogers Company

When William T. Graham founded the W.T. Rogers Company in 1949, he started small. "I put $15 in a bank account, and I haven't invested any more money since," he says. "I started on the $15 and made it grow."

At the time, Graham was still

chased the raw materials at retail stores and made the brushes in his basement. Initially, the entrepreneur also kept all the books and did all the selling. "I had to demonstrate it to sell it," he recalls. "If I demonstrated how to use the brush, it sold. But it didn't sell just

finishing law school. Kuypers, who is now the second-largest stockholder in Rogers and chief executive officer, took over the books and for a time operated the entire company from a desk drawer on the third floor of his campus fraternity house. Graham, with his skill

W.T. Rogers Company chief executive officer, Jerry Kuypers (left), and chairman of the board, Bill Graham (right), celebrate 40 years in business.

Employee teamwork makes good things happen at W.T. Rogers Company.

working as a branch manager for the Underwood Company, but he soon resigned to devote full time to his fledgling office supplies venture. "I guess I'm a good risk-taker," he says. "It wasn't too practical to quit Underwood when I had kids and house payments. I had to earn money every day because I couldn't borrow it."

Graham, who is now the privately held company's chairman of the board, started his business with a single product: a brush used to clean typewriters. He pur-

sitting on the shelf without any fancy packaging."

The brushes sold so well that Graham decided to expand his product line. He devised a rubber underlay to go under a typewriter; the pad both muffled the sound and kept the machine from slipping around on the desk. "I was the first person to use rubber instead of felt for these," Graham says. The typewriter pad sold for $1.25, and "it was a hot item." As with the brushes, Graham bought the raw materials and cut up and trimmed the product by hand as orders came in.

Jerome H. Kuypers, who had an accounting degree from the University of Wisconsin, joined the company in 1950 while he was

in product development and sales, and Kuypers, with his talent for organization and finance, formed the team that built the present organization.

The firm's policy from the beginning was that "everything is guaranteed to sell; we'll take it back if it doesn't," according to Graham. The policy turned out to be an effective sales tool, and W.T. Rogers grew steadily. The company had sales of $42,000 its first year in business. Sales grew to $160,000 the second year. "We made money every year with the exception of one," Graham says.

W.T. Rogers catalog covers representing 40 years in the business, from 1949 to 1989.

W.T. Rogers has continued to grow. The company had sales of more than $40 million in 1989—a 250-percent growth rate over the preceding four years. The product line has grown as well; today Rogers sells 1,800 different products. It manufactures approximately half of those itself, and the rest are manufactured by subcontractors and sold under the Rogers label.

The firm today employs 289 people and manufactures and sells a wide variety of products to help organize business offices and home offices. "We provide, manufacture, and sell nearly everything you need to organize the office and home office that isn't something you sit on or plug in," according to Jonathan Barry, president and chief operating officer.

W.T. Rogers manufactures plastic, injection-molded desk-top office accessories, school supplies, and also imports commodity office products such as paper clips, rubber bands, and staplers. Proprietary products (the company holds seven design and process patents and has applied for 18 more) include the Stak-ette® letter tray and the nine-item Klodt™ designer line.

The Stak-ette® letter tray is the firm's best-selling item: 2 million letter trays each year. Rogers also produces a full line of other high-quality plastic desk-top products in "fashion colors."

The corporation serves both the retail office products market and the consumer mass market. As a mid-size manufacturer with a national sales force, together with an East Coast distribution center, Rogers can respond quickly to market demand. For example, it consistently ships to dealers and smaller wholesalers within three days of receiving an order; next-day shipment is not uncommon.

"W.T. Rogers is one of the larger out-shippers from Madison," according to Graham. "We export products from Madison and import dollars back to Madison," he adds. "Our payroll is $5 million-plus a year." Graham is particularly pleased with the firm's foreign sales. "Unlike most companies, we're manufacturing in Wisconsin and selling in Mexico."

The organization is keeping its injection-molding manufacturing base in South Madison, while also expanding into a newly constructed 221,000-square-foot warehouse and manufacturing facility on Madison's far southeast end. "I love Wisconsin," explains Graham. "It's a beautiful state and a fine place to live, with a healthy economic climate, a good educational system, and we have a high-quality and stable work force from South Madison."

Graham has not always lived in Madison; he is originally from Georgia, but left to serve in the Air Force during World War II. Shot down over Germany twice, he was a prisoner of war for 13 months until he and his fellow prisoners were liberated by Patton's army. Graham ended up in Madison when he was discharged at Truax Field. "I loved Madison and stayed on," he says.

Graham named his venture W.T. Rogers Company, rather than W.T. Graham Company so he wouldn't have to let the world know that he was the only employee. There have been a lot of changes in the 40 years since then. Today all four of his children—Judy, Patti, Susie, and Bob—work at the company, as well as nearly 300 other employees. All employees have the opportunity to become owners through the Employee Stock Option Plan (ESOP), which was formed in 1988. No one who buys in today, however, is likely to make the kind of return on investment that Graham realized from the $15 he plunked down 40 years ago.

Desk accessories in W.T. Rogers' Southwest Shades™ fashion colors for home and office interiors.

Tracor Northern

Tracor Northern, which develops and manufactures high-technology instruments known worldwide for their accuracy, speed, and display capabilities, is not located in the greater Madison area by accident. When its predecessor company, Nuclear Data, moved to suburban Chicago, several employees were so firm in their resolve to stay in the Madison area that they staged a sit-down strike. When that did not work, two employees, Bill Buffo and Robert Schumann, founded the Northern Scientific Company in 1964. Northern Scientific was sold to Tracor Inc. (an international company employing more than 11,000 people and with revenues in excess of $700 million) in 1966. Westmark Systems, a financial holding company, purchased Tracor Inc. in 1987.

Today Tracor Northern designs and manufactures X-ray microanalysis, image-processing, confocal microscopy, and neurodiagnostic monitoring systems for industrial, university, and medical laboratory use. Tracor Northern's 85,000-square-foot facility in Middleton, Wisconsin, serves as the headquarters for the entire Tracor Instruments Group that also includes facilities in California, Texas, and Europe.

Robert L. Smialek, vice-president of the Tracor Instruments Group, thinks that Tracor Northern will continue to thrive in its challenging marketing niche because of the company's emphasis on research and development. "More than 40 of our 300 employees in Middleton are in research and development," Smialek says. He adds, though, that such a heavy emphasis on developing new products is essential in order to be competitive. "Because it's such a high-tech field, we have to grow to compete," Smialek says. "So we listen to our customers."

The firm develops both entirely new products, and enhanced features and new applications for existing systems. Recent new products included the first fully integrated Automated Digital Electron Microscope (known as ADEM), the Tandem Scanning Reflected Light Microscope, and the EEGLE, which

This operator is shown analyzing the chemical composition of a microchip using one of Tracor's X-ray microanalysis systems. The monitor at left is the X-ray microanalysis monitor; on the right is the image of the sample. This technology makes it possible to determine the chemical composition of the sample. The image corresponds to the actual physical configuration of the sample.

monitors neurological activity during surgery. Other Tracor Northern instruments are used on shipboard, in crime laboratories, in product-testing laboratories, and in pollution-control facilities. In 1987 Tracor Northern received *R&D Magazine*'s prestigious national R&D 100 Award for ADEM.

Tracor Northern instruments are used in a wide variety of locations. "We're a global company," Smialek says. Though the firm is settled in Middleton, half of its sales are outside the continental United States. Still Tracor Northern retains its local ties to the Madison area. "We have strong ties to UW-Madison, both personally and professionally," Smialek says. "And our company benefits from the strong work ethic that is prevalent in Madison and the surrounding area."

Employees of Tracor Northern gathered outside one of Tracor's two locations in Middleton in the fall of 1988.

Placon

One of the largest and most advanced custom thermoforming plants in the country is located on the outskirts of Madison. Founded by Thomas Mohs in 1966, Placon now employs 260 people at its computer-driven headquarters on a 20-acre site. In 1969 Placon occupied 6,000 square feet on the same site it now occupies; a new addition, completed in 1988, brings the facility to a total of 180,000 square feet.

Mohs, who is president and chief executive officer of the company, attributes Placon's success partially to its location in Madison. "We're very fortunate to be located where we are," Mohs says. "We have a stable and highly qualified employee base, which is important

Placon's manufacturing facility is one of the most modern and advanced custom thermoforming plants in the nation.

both to me personally and to the company. I'm very proud of the people we have working here."

Placon manufactures custom-thermoformed products with some stock product lines. Thermoforming is the process of converting plastic from a flat sheet in roll form into light-gauge, lightweight products. The majority of the products

Placon makes are sold to manufacturers and are used as packaging materials.

The privately held company has three major product lines: custom light-gauge thermoforming (which makes up the majority of its business), BlisterBox® transparent display packages, and BonFaire® disposable food-serving systems. Placon manufactures packaging used in the consumer, food, medical, and catering industries. Blister-Boxes®, for example, come in 40 stock sizes that are used for packaging a wide variety of products, including office products, fasteners, fishing paraphernalia, and hardware. BonFaire® products, which include a variety of snack and full meal trays with clear hinged covers, are used by caterers serving the airline, rail, cruise ship, and bus industries.

Placon's size enables the company to offer its customers several advantages. "Because of our relatively large size in the industry, Placon can support and offer an extensive product design and project

Placon's computer-controlled machines have been specially adapted to allow for a very short tooling change time, which allows Placon to run a large number of different parts.

development capability," Mohs says. Placon utilizes state-of-the-art computer-aided design (CAD) to configure complex shapes that could not be otherwise machined. The firm's designers, engineers, and marketing staff work together with clients to design functional and aesthetically appealing products. In addition, Placon offers customers services such as labeling and assembling to support the basic thermoforming product line.

When Mohs founded Placon in a garage in 1966, he purchased the first model ever sold of a machine that played a major part in revolutionizing the plastics-thermoforming industry. That machine, and others purchased since then, employ the thermoforming process, which utilizes both pressure and a vacuum to form a continuous sheet of heated plastic into various products. The process enables a plastic product to have very thin walls and a uniform thickness, both desirable traits in packaging materials.

CHAPTER NINE

Business and Professions

G reater Madison's professional community
brings a wealth of service,
ability, and insight to
the community.

Photo by Brent Nicastro

Greater Madison Chamber of Commerce

"We could just as easily be called the Dane County Chamber of Commerce," says Robert W. "Bob" Brennan, president of the Greater Madison Chamber of Commerce. "We cover all of Dane County, from Stoughton to Middleton, but, of course, Madison is the name most people recognize." Brennan, a lifelong resident of Madison, is an enthusiastic booster of the greater Madison area. "Madison is a city of opportunity," he says. "We have a world-class university, a beautiful physical setting, and a hardworking, well-educated work force."

Madison's lakes are what most people notice first; the city is located on the shores of four large lakes, and many others are nearby. The park system is also impressive. There are miles of cross-country ski trails and bicycle paths within city limits. The Vilas Park Zoo has free admission and is located in an easily accessible city park. The University of Wisconsin-Madison Arboretum is a 12,600-acre outdoor ecological laboratory that provides living examples of the major plant communities—prairies, woodlands, marshes, and ponds. The arboretum's free skiing and hiking trails and nature tours are open to the public.

Madison's many cultural facilities include 27 theaters that feature entertainment ranging from avant-garde cinema to concert pianists. The downtown Madison Civic Center and the Dane County Coliseum

host events ranging from fairs, rodeos, and carnivals to drama, opera, and rock concerts. Other attractions include Madison's 80-member symphony orchestra, the 35-piece Wisconsin Chamber Orchestra, and the American Players Theater in Spring Green.

Art Fair in the Square takes place on the Capitol Square in Madison and is one of the many cultural community events that Madison hosts. Photo by Bruce Fritz

The greater Madison area is also thriving economically. "We have one of the greatest communities in the world," Dane County executive Richard J. Phelps says. "Dane County is a wonderful place in which to live, to do business, and to raise families. Our county, made up of 60 diverse communities, has a world-class university, a highly motivated and skilled work force, and the best farmland in the state." Area business, education, labor, and local government leaders

recently mapped out an economic development plan called the Dane County Economic Summit. And Sematech, the research consortium for the U.S. semiconductor industry, recently selected UW-Madison as one of 10 Centers of Excellence.

The Greater Madison Chamber of Commerce is a key partner in the creation of economic initiatives. "Business, labor, government, and the university all share a deep-seated commitment to serving the best interests of our community," Brennan says. "Working together, we can create a climate conducive to economic growth and stability." The chamber, which is affiliated with the National Chamber of Commerce, has a full-time paid staff. Its board of directors, made up of area business people, is responsible for the various programs and general direction of the chamber. More than 1,000 Dane County firms, representing all parts of the business spectrum, are members of the chamber.

Warzyn Engineering Inc.

cal staff and appropriate information systems in order to meet clients' expectations.

The Warzyn staff has professionals in many disciplines, allowing the company to provide a full range of environmental services encompassing the study, design, and construction phases of a project. With its resources the firm is able to respond effectively and in a timely manner to a client's needs. Major activities

In 35 years Warzyn Engineering Inc. has grown from a modest beginning to become one of the top design firms in the country. The company's first two employees (founder Willard W. Warzyn and his wife, Jeanne) worked in a 600-square-foot office in the basement of a Park Street office building in Madison. Today the award-winning broad-spectrum technology firm employs nearly 300 people in several locations, including Madison's new University Research Park, which was a project of Warzyn's, and also in Milwaukee; Chicago; Detroit; and New York. Plans are also being considered for expansion to the Philadelphia area.

Warzyn specializes in developing solutions to complex and unusual environmental engineering problems. The company offers unique and innovative expertise in planning, analysis, design, and construction management services, although initially it specialized in civil and geotechnical engineering.

In the 30 years since its founding, Warzyn Engineering Inc. has become one of the top design firms in the country and employs more than 325 people in five locations.

Major company programs include environmental assessments, industrial waste handling, and solid and hazardous waste management. Warzyn also offers services of a large analytical laboratory that is located in-house in Madison. It also provides remediation and asbestos services. Warzyn's clients include both private entities and public-sector agencies.

"Three fundamental problem-solving principles govern Warzyn's approach," notes William Thayer, president of the company. "We develop a functional, cost-effective solution. We meet project schedules—and we complete our efforts within budget." Thayer adds that every project is assigned a knowledgeable project manager, who is supported by trained techni-

can be performed in-house in order to enhance confidentiality, quality, communications, and cost control. Such flexibility and efficiency are always crucial, since work scopes and client needs can change during a project.

Warzyn is actively involved in the Madison market as well. One of its most prominent projects is something most Madisonians take for granted: the Monona Causeway. Willard Warzyn points to the 3,500-foot causeway as one of the highlights of his career. "One of my most satisfying projects was the soil borings, geotechnical analysis, and successful construction of the hydraulically placed roadway fill over more than 40 feet of very soft compressible organic silt and clay," says Warzyn, who is the founder of the privately held company.

Warzyn points out how successful the Monona Causeway has been. "When the causeway, known as John Nolen Drive, was com-

pleted in 1965, there had never before been direct access to the capitol area from Madison's growing south side." Today few people who drive on the road built over water realize what a technical feat it represents. "Because of the soft lake bottom, the embankment has settled more than 14 feet since it was placed, unknown to those who travel the roadway," Warzyn says.

Many of Warzyn's designs are innovative and progressive. The company has been a front runner in the field of environmental studies and design, which now accounts for approximately 75 percent of its revenue. The City of Madison has been a nationwide leader in addressing problems of solid-waste disposal, and Warzyn's early expertise in the environmen-

tal area grew out of its work for the City of Madison. A notable example is the company's design of the Duzinski Resource Recovery Center to convert solid waste to fuel sources and current efforts with Dane County to solve the area's solid waste disposal problems.

The company is actively involved with community agencies such as the Madison Enterprise Center and the United Way of Dane County. Staff members teach short courses on technical subjects at UW-Madison and give technical presentations and expert testimony on matters affecting the community. In recognition of its high-quality engineering and design innovations, Warzyn Engineering Inc. has received a number of technical awards.

Viking Insurance Company of Wisconsin

Madison's west side has been home to the corporate headquarters of a unique insurance company since its founding in 1971. Viking Insurance Company serves what is known as the "nonstandard" automobile and specialty insurance markets. Nonstandard auto insurance clients include drivers who are considered higher risks than other drivers mainly due to poor driving records, but sometimes also because of other factors such as lack of driving experience or high-performance automobiles.

"We provide a valuable service in the marketplace," says Viking's president, Timothy L. Brown. "We bridge the gap between the nonstandard and the standard or pre-

ferred world." But, while Viking's customer base of insured clients is as loyal as those of most insurance companies, it maintains a much different relationship due to its unique product. Viking's insureds tend to move back into the standard market as soon as their circumstances permit. In fact, nine months is the average length of a Viking Insurance policy.

"Our objective as a company is to clearly differentiate ourselves as a nonstandard specialty carrier—not a substandard carrier," Brown says. "We are insurance professionals dealing in the nonstandard marketplace. We provide a quality product and pride ourselves on the quality of our service."

Viking Insurance Company's new office building in Madison.

Xerox Credit Corporation, and other financial joint-venture operations.

Viking has found a lot of opportunity in the nonstandard specialty market. Nonstandard auto and motorcycle premiums available nationwide currently total $7 billion per year, and the market is growing rapidly. In addition to the nonstandard automobile coverages, which account for about 95 percent of its business, Viking also offers various specialty insurance lines, including motorcycle coverage, short-term travel and accident policies, and sportsman packages (including hunting, fishing, and related camping activities).

Viking currently does business in 16 states: Arizona, Arkansas, California, Idaho, Illinois, Indiana, Iowa, Missouri, Nebraska, New Mexico, North Dakota, Oregon, South Dakota, Texas, Washington, and Wisconsin. The company has five regional offices: Irvine, California; Indianapolis, Indiana; Salem, Oregon; Austin, Texas; and Madison, Wisconsin (also the location of the home office).

Pictured here are (back row, left to right) Fred Craig, vice-president/marketing; Timothy Brown, president; Donald Ringham, vice-president/human resources; (front row, left to right) James Cizek, vice-president/field administration; and Gregory Goodrich, vice-president, treasurer, and chief financial officer.

Viking Insurance has been recognized for that commitment to quality. The company is rated "excellent" by A.M. Best Company. Viking is a member company of Xerox Financial Services, a network of corporations including Van Kampen Merritt, Furman Selz,

Viking is looking to expand into several more states while maintaining its dominance of current markets. "Our aim is to be one of the top one or two nonstandard companies in the markets we

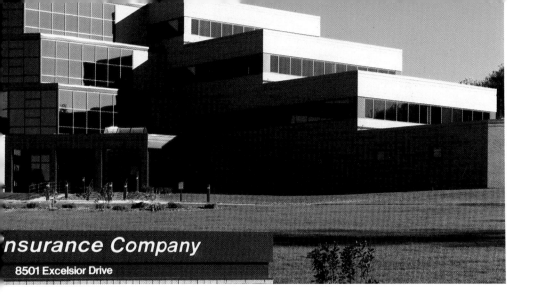

...nsurance Company
8501 Excelsior Drive

serve," says Brown, who joined the company in 1986. "I am confident we can do it."

Backing up Brown's confidence is a strong network of more than 7,000 independent agents who represent Viking to the people who buy insurance. "Technically, our customer is the independent agent. We are dedicated to the independent agency system and have a real commitment to those people," Brown says. He believes that one of the strengths of the company is the caliber of agents it attracts and retains. "We have high-quality standards," Brown says. "We choose high-quality agents. We are not a take-all-comers company."

Viking is able to attract good agents because it offers them service commitments and product features not available with other carriers, according to Brown. "We have always prided ourselves on our service to agents," he says. "That's been a hallmark of Viking Insurance since the inception of our corporation." He particularly singles out the timeliness and quality of Viking claim settlements. "Those clearly separate us from the competition."

Viking currently employs more than 500 people in the 16 states it serves; there are 150 people in the Madison office. As the company has grown, it has confirmed its commitment to remaining in Wisconsin. "There's a healthy insurance environment in the state," Brown says.

"Wisconsin offers a strong economy, good employees, and an attractive regulatory environment." Viking has completed a 62,000-square-foot home office on the far west side of Madison that reinforces the firm's commitment to Wisconsin.

The new building, which is 2.5 times larger than the former facility, was designed and built by local organizations. The architect was Potter, Lawson Architects; the builder was J.H. Findorff and Sons. The new facility was designed to offer plenty of room for expansion during the next 10 years.

Viking is involved in a variety of community service activities, including public service announcements urging safe driving. The firm and its employees also provide ongoing support for community service organizations such as the United Way of Dane County, the Red Cross, and the Four Lakes Council of the Boy Scouts of America, as well as special events such as Madison's Festival of the Lakes.

Viking Insurance Company was founded by two brothers, Don and Bob Anderson, who chose the name "Viking" because of their Scandinavian heritage, and Bob was a classmate and good friend of Bud Grant, former head coach of the Minnesota Vikings football team. Crum and Forster acquired Viking in 1982; the firm is now a member of the Xerox Financial Services Organization.

The Viking Insurance management team includes (back row, left to right) Lewis Winter, vice-president/operations; Collins Avery, vice-president/claims; Gregory Madson, vice-president/pricing/government affairs; (front row, left to right) Craig Lochner, vice-president/controller; and Ronald Johnson, vice-president/management systems. Not pictured: Robert Wilkes, vice-president/ underwriting.

111

Rural Insurance Companies

Rural's most prominent local real estate investment is Old Sauk Trails Park, a 406-acre high-quality office/research park.

"Well over half of our 600 employees have worked for Rural Insurance more than five years, and half of those have worked here longer than 10 years," says Donald Haldeman, president of the Rural Insurance Companies. "The longevity of our employees reflects the stability of the Madison work force. We have both stability and quality here. There may on the surface appear to be a lower-cost employee in other markets, but the quality of Madison's work force is intangible and irreplaceable."

Rural has been located in Madison since it was founded by the Wisconsin Farm Bureau in 1934 to provide vehicle insurance for farmers, a market larger insurance companies were not interested in servicing at the time. In 1949 Rural Security Life Insurance Company

Located in a contemporary landmark structure, Rural Insurance provides a complete portfolio of life, health, auto, home, farm, and business insurance tailored to the needs of Farm Bureau members, individuals, and businesses.

was organized, adding life and health insurance lines; today Rural offers a complete portfolio of life, health, auto, home, farm, and business insurance tailored to the needs of Farm Bureau members, individuals, and businesses. The companies have grown tremendously; in a recent 10-year period total policies grew from 75,000 to 250,000, and premium income for 1989 was more than $120 million.

As Rural has expanded, its home office has moved and grown, from a brick storefront on Williamson Street in 1934 to the stunning contemporary landmark building erected in 1970 on Mineral Point Road across from West Towne. Rural is committed to Madison and Wisconsin. "We have a stake in Madison's future," says Lyman R. Frazier, Rural's executive vice-president. "We've served Wisconsin families for more than 50 years, and we expect to be here another 50." Frazier adds that newcomers seem equally fond of Madison. "Madison's quality of life makes it

awfully easy to recruit professional employees from outside the area."

"Rural is recognized as a quality provider of insurance services—an achievement due to the dedicated teamwork of employees, agents, and agency managers in the home office, claims offices, and service centers," Haldeman says.

Rural's commitment to Wisconsin is reflected in the firm's investments; its real estate portfolio, for example, is made up of at least 80 percent Wisconsin properties. Several well-known Madison developments, such as Westgate Mall and Whitney Square, are owned by Rural. "We see our real estate investments as a way to help invigorate the community," Frazier says.

Serving Wisconsin families for more than 50 years, Rural Insurance is committed to Madison and Wisconsin.

"When we bought Westgate Mall in 1973, for example, we renovated a tired old shopping center both exterior and interior, and made it an asset to the community."

Rural's most prominent local real estate investment is Old Sauk Trails Park, a 406-acre high-quality office/research park. "Working with the city, we put together an environmentally advanced development unlike any other," Lyman says. "Old Sauk Trails Park has more green space, more manufacturing and warehousing restrictions, larger setbacks, less blacktop, and more plantings than is usual in a development."

The office/research park features stands of oak trees, meandering roads, duck ponds, a jogging trail, and views of a golf course, Lake Medota, and the state capitol. Other amenities include a hotel and a private day-care center. De-

spite its rural atmosphere, Old Sauk Trails Park has direct access to the West Beltline, which leads directly to Madison's interstate highway system.

Promotion of Old Sauk Trails Park is being pursued by the Gialamas Company. Early development of the office/research park includes offices and facilities for First Wisconsin National Bank, the American Automobile Association of Wisconsin, Budgetel, Mattson Instrument, Viking Insurance, the Wisconsin Milk Marketing Board, Wisconsin Mutual Insurance Company, RMT, Heurikon, State Farm Insurance, Joiner Associates, Treehouse Day

Care, Farm Plan Insurance, General Telephone Company, CUNA Mutual Insurance, and A&R Editions. Additional facilities house numerous other professional and technical operations.

The Wisconsin Farm Bureau was founded in 1920 by farm families across the state who felt a need to work together to build a strong rural voice in public policy issues that affect farmers. Today the federation membership is represented by country and city families—more than 55,000 member-families strong. There are more than 3 million farm bureau members nationwide.

The federation represents Wisconsin farmers, individuals, and businesses, including those who produce hogs, cattle, poultry, dairy products, vegetables, grains, and fruits such as cherries, apples, strawberries, and cranberries.

"There's a lot of rural in Wisconsin and a lot of Wisconsin in Rural," says Haldeman, who owns a 500-acre farm in Monroe County, in addition to his leadership role.

A stable and dependable work force is one of the many assets that puts Rural Insurance above its competition.

Mead & Hunt, Consulting Engineers

The 200,000-square-foot Leprino Foods/ Michigan Milk Producers Association facility in Allendale, Michigan, is considered the "largest mozzarella cheese plant in the world." Mead & Hunt led complete design of the facility.

"The first glimpse that a lot of people get of Madison and Dane County is our work at the airport," says Leo C. Bussan, president of Mead & Hunt, Consulting Engineers. But once they've safely landed, just a one-day drive throughout the area would put any traveler in contact with hundreds of other projects undertaken by the engineering/architectural firm.

One could begin in the heart of Madison with a ride past design work at Camp Randall Stadium, the county fairgrounds, and the University of Wisconsin's heating plant, then move on to major subdivisions such as Cross Country Heights in Verona, manufacturing/ office complexes such as the Ohmeda medical products facility on Interstate 90, and surrounding communities where municipal engineering projects such as streets, storm sewers, and wastewater-treatment plants are a constant. There would be stops at village halls, parks, shopping centers, and perhaps Sun Prairie's Evora Lodge, a senior citizens' apartment complex with an award-winning design. It would be one long, but very interesting, day.

"We're proud of our visibility in Dane County, as well as our engineering contributions throughout the state and country," says Bussan. Visibility and notoriety are something Mead & Hunt has known from its founding in 1900 by Daniel W. Mead, an internationally recognized pioneer in hydroelectric and hydraulic engineering. Professor Mead led many of the Midwest's first hydroelectric projects, while building an increasingly multidisciplined firm.

True to Mead's vision, the firm has remained strong in the area of hydroelectric development, while also becoming a recognized expert in dairy and food plants, airports, highways and bridges, building systems, and municipal services. Staff members include civil engineers, electrical engineers, hydrologists, environmental specialists, planners, structural and mechanical engineers, architects, surveyors, soils engineers, sanitary engineers, and construction inspectors.

Current work in the Dane County area includes design of a well system for the UW-Foundation's championship 18-hole golf course near Verona; a pedestrian/bicyclist underpass for the West Beltline; a 350-lot, residential subdivision in Madison; and expansion of a major metal-casting operation in Madison.

Perhaps Mead & Hunt's most prominent recent project in Dane County was the infrastructure for Middleton's new Greenway Center. The 100-plus-acre development includes a 300-room Holiday Inn, convention center, six-story office/ banking building, shopping center, and retail complex. Project management was provided as well as facility design of street, sewer, and water systems; bidding assistance;

Runways, taxiways, aprons, and airport security programs are just a few of the projects carried out by Mead & Hunt since 1965 in its continuous work for the Dane County Regional Airport.

and construction administration.

Transportation projects—such as development of that most visible Dane County Regional Airport—have been an important part of Mead & Hunt's services since the 1940s. More than 31 airports have been improved by Mead & Hunt. At several of them, the firm serves as airport engineer. At the Dane County Regional Airport, Mead & Hunt has engineered nearly all new construction of, and improvements to, runways, taxiways, and aprons since 1965.

Highways and bridges have been designed by the firm in more than 50 of Wisconsin's 72 counties. As with other work, Mead & Hunt is capable of taking highway and bridge projects from the preliminary study and design phase through the construction phase.

Since Mead & Hunt is located in Wisconsin, the nation's dairyland and an area known for its vast water resources, it's not surprising the firm has honed its exper-

Development of the 80-acre Ohmeda headquarters and manufacturing facility in Madison was led by Mead & Hunt. Mead & Hunt has continued to provide engineering services for the major manufacturer of medical products.

tise in water resources and dairy and food plants.

Hydroelectric, levee, and dam projects have been undertaken in such diverse locations as Pennsylvania, Virginia, North Dakota, and Alabama. Professional citations for engineering excellence have been earned for such innovative projects as one of the nation's first siphon-penstock hydroelectric plants.

As for dairy and food plant projects, Mead & Hunt has continuously expanded its services and geographic coverage since the early 1940s, when work for Wisconsin's dairy plants and cooperatives began. Today, in addition to its continuing relationship with such major producers as Wisconsin Dairies Cooperative and Associated Milk Producers, Inc. (AMPI), Mead & Hunt has served such varied clients as Oscar Mayer Foods, Ocean Spray Cranberries, Kraft, and Sysco Foods. In Michigan, the firm recently designed what is considered the world's largest mozzarella cheese plant for Leprino Foods Company and Michigan

The 200-acre Cross Country Heights subdivision in Verona, southwest of Madison, was planned and platted by Mead & Hunt in a series of nine additions over a 10-year period. More growth is still expected for the 400-lot private development, which includes homes, apartments, town houses, and parks.

Milk Producers Association.

"For some of our clients in the food industry, we've worked at every plant they have," Bussan says. "They could find engineers that are local, but they know us and know our service, so we do work for them all over." Indeed, Mead & Hunt has designed dairy and food plants nationwide, from Massachusetts and Maryland, to Missouri, Utah, and California.

Despite the wide geographic range of its clients, Mead & Hunt intends to keep its headquarters in Madison. "We look at Madison as a very desirable community to live and work in," Bussan says. He cites factors such as "the clean environment, good working conditions, good recreational opportunities, and the excellent engineering school at UW-Madison, which is a good source of employees for us." Plus, says Bussan, "Madison is centrally located in the Midwest and in the United States. We don't have a difficult time going places."

First Wisconsin National Bank of Madison

When the forerunner of the First Wisconsin National Bank of Madison—then called Dane County Bank—applied for a charter as a national bank in 1863 (nine years after it was founded), the federal government required the bank's cashier to travel to Washington, D.C., carrying $50,000 in gold in a satchel to prove the bank's assets.

The bank has undergone some fairly minor name changes in the intervening years, acquiring its present name in 1970. The change in its assets, on the other hand, has been phenomenal: From $50,000 in the 1860s, the bank's assets have grown to surpass $565 million in the late 1980s. Today First Wisconsin-Madison is the oldest and one of the largest banks in Madison; it is the fifth-largest bank in the state.

A favorite saying at First Wisconsin is that the bank is made up of "professionals helping people." "We are in the service business, and the key element that distinguishes us from our competition is people," says James Lang, president and chief executive officer. "We are leading the way in developing a staff that is customer oriented and professional, who can work effectively with architects, business owners, attorneys, young people, seniors, cab drivers, whoever our customer may be. We aggressively analyze what our customers need and respond quickly and creatively."

One of the prime examples of First Wisconsin's service to customers is its network of banking locations placed within minutes of anyone in the greater metropolitan area. The offices reflect new concepts in the delivery of financial services, including expertise in numerous fields and dedicated, personally assigned bankers.

The bank's Trust Division is by far the largest in the area with more than 150 employees managing in excess of $2 billion in assets. Whether serving businesses or individuals, the trust market is highly results oriented. Investment performance has gained national recognition and ranking, a prime reason, along with customer service, for the bank's unprecedented growth.

The area of Business Banking has always been a strong suit for First Wisconsin. Under the philosophy of professional service, it has gained a reputation as a valuable source of financial advice, as well as a credit source. The bank's $7-billion parent company, Firstar, deepens that ability and specialization with its staff and the assets that the family of Firstar banks throughout Wisconsin, Illinois, and Minnesota represent.

But it's not size or experience that distinguishes First Wisconsin National Bank of Madison; it's the staff of outstanding professionals prepared to help people meet their financial needs.

First Wisconsin-Madison's distinctive glass building, located on the Capitol Square in Madison. The First Wisconsin Plaza (completed in 1974) provides banking, office, and shopping facilities. Designed with energy conservation in mind, the unusual building offers customers and employees beautiful views of downtown Madison and the surrounding lakes.

First Wisconsin National Bank of Madison is the oldest and one of the largest banks in Madison—it is the fifth-largest bank in the state. Photo by Harriet Vander Meer

Lathrop & Clark

Lathrop & Clark is a full-service law firm. Its areas of particular specialization include the legal fields of intellectual property, business (corporate practice and labor from the management side), banking, tax, commercial, real estate (including shopping center representation, site acquisition, annexation, zoning, and major project development), and estate planning (including legal audits to help new Wisconsin residents consider the implications of the state's marital property law).

Lathrop & Clark's long-established specialty in intellectual property services, including patent, trademark, and copyright law, has enabled it to serve many Madison high-technology companies (a number of which are associated in some way with UW-Madison). About 20 percent of the firm is made up of attorneys with a technical background, including mechanical engineering, electrical

A teamwork approach brings appropriate expertise to each client matter.

engineering, computers, food science, and biotechnology.

"Lathrop & Clark has been involved in patent filings for inventions ranging from DNA and

Personal concern for clients is central to the law practice of Lathrop & Clark.

bacteria to plants, animals, computer software, and digital signal processing," says Ted Long, partner.

"There are a lot of things that we can get patents on today that would have been science fiction 10 years ago."

Major clients of the firm include Nicolet Instrument Corporation, American Family Mutual Insurance Company, First Federal Savings Bank, the Wiscon-

sin Association of School Boards, the Wisconsin Alumni Research Foundation, Research Products Corporation, and the CUNA Mutual Insurance Group.

The firm's employees are active in the community. Members of Lathrop & Clark have served as president or chairman of the United Way of Dane County, Madison Community Foundation, Methodist Health Services Corporation, Downtown Madison Rotary Club, Madison Rotary Foundation, and Madison Professional Men's Club.

Members of the firm are also active in professional groups and have served as president or chairman of the State Bar of Wisconsin, Wisconsin Intellectual Property Law Association, Dane County Bar Association, Wisconsin Bar Foundation, and American Bar Association Subcommittee on Patenting Higher Life Forms. Members of the firm have also served on subcommittees advising the Wisconsin Legislature on technical corrections to the Wisconsin corporation law and the marital property law.

Lathrop & Clark and its predecessor firms have been well established in Madison since 1905. In addition to its headquarters in Madison, the firm maintains branch offices in Poynette, Lodi, and Belleville, Wisconsin.

Building Greater Madison

From concept to completion, Madison's building industry and real estate professionals shape tomorrow's skyline.

Photo by Bruce Fritz

J.H. Findorff & Son Inc.

"If you hung pictures of all the buildings we built in Madison, it would look like we built most of the city," says Kenneth J. Kruska, president of J.H. Findorff & Son Inc. "We've been builders of Madison since 1890."

In the 100 years since its founding, Findorff employees have constructed an impressive portion of the urban architecture of Madison, from small projects such as the Chamber of Commerce Building and the Olbrich Botanical Complex to the University of Wisconsin Medical Center, the largest structure ever built for the State of Wisconsin. "We don't consider any job too small, and nothing in Madison is too large," Kruska says. "Our project budgets range from $10,000 to $50 million."

Findorff constructed many Madison landmarks. Corporate office buildings erected by Findorff include Madison Newspapers, the Oscar Mayer Office Building, and RAYOVAC World Headquarters. Projects at the University of Wisconsin-Madison include the UW Medical Center, the McClain Athletic Facility, and the Wisconsin Alumni Research Foundation (WARF). Findorff has also constructed many insurance company and trade association buildings, including structures for the Credit Union National Association (CUNA), CUNA Mutual Insurance Company, General Casualty Insurance, Rural Insurance, National Guardian Life, Wisconsin Education Association Council (WEAC), and WEA Insurance Trust (WEAIT).

Other Findorff projects in Madison include GEF 1 and GEF 2 (the State of Wisconsin's General Executive Office Facilities), the Hilldale Shopping Mall, and the Madison Area Technical College (MATC). The Bear Exhibits, Sea Otter Exhibit, South American rain forest, penguin display, and the Herpetarium at Madison's Henry Vilas Zoo are among some of Findorff's more unique projects.

Elsewhere in Wisconsin, Findorff has constructed the Sentry Insurance World Headquarters in Stevens Point, the Trane Engineering Building in La Crosse, and the Henry Reuss Federal Plaza, Froedtert Memorial Lutheran Hospital, the Medical College of Wisconsin, and the Milwaukee Theater District, all in Milwaukee.

Findorff's willingness to take on a wide variety of construction projects is one of the keys to its success, according to Curt Hastings, vice-president. "A lot of contractors want to build your $10-million building, but when you want them to move a few walls, they say, 'We don't do that.' As a complete service contractor, we will do follow-up work and make renovations for our customers, even to the point of using our custom mill work shop where craftsmen construct detail work such as specialty moldings, doors, conference tables, and cabinets."

Although Findorff obtains much of its work by competitive bidding, an equal amount is negotiated directly with building owners. "Many owners prefer to have Findorff on the team early, preparing budgets and advising the architect, rather than waiting for bids to come in only to find out the project is over budget, the plans are complete, and it is too late to make

Credit Union Center.

St. Marys Hospital Ambulatory Surgery.

changes," says Hastings. "This is especially true of our many repeat customers. Often, we get the first job by competitive bid, the owner likes our people and our work, and he comes directly to us for future projects." Findorff provides these services through both Construction Management and Design Build.

Kruska believes that two of Findorff's particular strengths are accurate budgeting and scheduling. Findorff has a large staff of experienced project managers who can give early, accurate estimates from very preliminary drawings. These estimates are developed by Findorff's project managers through the use of an extensive data base of past project costs. In addition, the company has developed its own computerized estimating, cost accounting, and scheduling systems that Kruska believes are better than anything that is commercially available. This expertise in estimating based on preliminary plans makes it easier for Findorff to come up with an early guaranteed price. Findorff's ability to track projects ac-

curately is also helpful later in the construction process. "An important part of construction, both for us and for the owner, is knowing where the job stands financially at any point in time," Kruska points out.

Findorff's unique computerized project-tracking systems also enable the company to make the best use of its large inventory of major equipment. The firm keeps control of its jobs by doing some of the services itself, including basic general trades such as concrete, structural steel, and drywall. In fact, Findorff is one of the largest drywall contractors in Wisconsin. As Kruska points out, "We can subcontract or not subcontract. Our skilled labor force together with our extensive equipment reserve provide many options."

Findorff just celebrated its 100th anniversary. "We're the only

major contractor in Madison that's been around that long," Kruska says. "But we're still every bit as young, aggressive, and competitive as we've ever been. We're an old firm but a young company. Our people are young in both age and thinking. And, of course, as our motto says, 'Companies Don't Build—People Build.'"

Despite the youth of Findorff's staff, there is very little turnover. Among the professional staff, there is almost zero turnover other than retirement. The three principal owners are themselves part of that tradition. Ken Kruska joined the firm in 1954, Gerd Zoller was hired in 1968, and Curt Hastings came aboard in 1970. The three of them

One East Main Street Office Building.

purchased the company from the Findorff family in 1981.

The firm is still located on the same site on West Wilson Street in downtown Madison where it was founded by John H. Findorff in 1890. Subsequent presidents of the company were Milton B. Findorff,

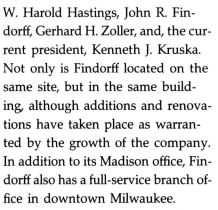

W. Harold Hastings, John R. Findorff, Gerhard H. Zoller, and, the current president, Kenneth J. Kruska. Not only is Findorff located on the same site, but in the same building, although additions and renovations have taken place as warranted by the growth of the company. In addition to its Madison office, Findorff also has a full-service branch office in downtown Milwaukee.

The locally owned, privately

U.W. Hospital and Clinics.

ica, including the Wisconsin and Milwaukee chapters, the Madison Home Builders Association, and the National Home Builders Association. The firm is also active in the community as shown by its support of the United Way of Dane County, Edgewood College, the University of

General Casualty Insurance.

Wisconsin-Madison Athletic Department, the Madison Civic Center, the Madison Art Center, the Four Lakes Council of Boy Scouts of America, Oakwood Village (retirement apartments), and the Greater Madison Chamber of Commerce.

J.H. Findorff & Son Inc.'s long tradition of quality building and service to its customers is a plus in the construction business. "You don't stay in this business unless you've done some things right," Hastings points out. "We have many repeat customers, and we pride ourselves on the quality of our service to our clients, both old and new."

held company has an average sales volume of $70 million per year and employs an average of 350 people. John R. Findorff, the grandson of founder John H. Findorff, is currently chairman of the board. Since 1987 all office employees participate in an employee stock ownership plan, the eventual goal being to have the firm entirely employee owned.

Findorff is active in several trade associations, including the Associated General Contractors of Amer-

RAYOVAC World Headquarters.

The Stark Company, Realtors

"We've sold more homes than any-body else in Dane County," says Phillip C. Stark, chairman of The Stark Company, Realtors, which was founded in 1908 by his grand-father, A.C. Stark, a Presbyterian minister. "We're by far and away the oldest residential real estate com-pany in the county."

Stark attributes much of the suc-cess of his company to its location. "Madison is a great place," he says. "I've traveled a lot and never found anything to begin to com-pare with it. I'm convinced that Dane County is one of the finest places in America to live." Stark cites three major reasons for his en-thusiasm: the physical environ-ment, the people, and the business climate.

"Just to say that Madison is beautiful isn't enough," Stark says. "Madison's beauty must be lived. Where else could you walk a few short blocks from the heart of the central business district and be in a lakeshore park on one of three dif-ferent lakes? And our rolling ter-rain and curved, tree-lined streets make attractive residential neighbor-hoods at all price levels."

Stark cites the people of Madi-son as another plus. "Madison is a young city; more than 40,000 stu-dents at the UW keep us that way." As for the business climate, Stark points to the "ultra-stable in-dustries" of government, the univer-sity, and other large businesses. "Property values have held well," Stark adds. "We find buyers and sellers of real estate happy with Madison."

The family-owned business, which employs more than 130 full-time salespeople and a support

The Stark Company has been instrumental in the residential development of Madison, including Nakoma (foreground).

staff of 20, has been a leader both in the real estate industry and in the Madison community.

Paul E. Stark (Phil's father and A.C.'s son) was one of the prime de-velopers of Nakoma and many other residential areas. Paul Stark was president of the National Associ-ation of Realtors in 1937, and Phil Stark served as treasurer of the na-tional association. Phil Stark's son, David, president of the firm, is a past president of the Greater Madison Board of Realtors. And, in response to the changing realities of financing resi-dential real estate, the Stark Company was the first realtor in town to open its own mortgage company.

The Stark Company, Realtors, has also been

very involved in the community over the years. Phil Stark, for exam-ple, has been president of the Down-town Madison Rotary Club and chairman of the board of the Greater Madison Chamber of Com-merce, as well as a leader in many other civic organizations. Says Stark, "It's my feeling that you can't really do business in a city like this and be just a taker—you must be a giver as well."

David and Phillip Stark, president and chair-man of the board, respectively.

Mardi O'Brien Real Estate, Inc.

Mardelle J. O'Brien's real estate career began in 1974 in Madison. Her real estate business has thrived, and O'Brien is a leader in the real estate field both locally and nationally.

"I believe in quality and service, and I believe in Madison and Dane County," says Mardelle J. O'Brien, president and owner of Mardi O'Brien Real Estate, Inc. "I think that the quality of life that we have here is superb. It's safe and it's a very clean community where people care about each other." Although O'Brien was brought up in Wisconsin, she lived for many years on the West Coast where, she says, "people have tons of acquaintances, but it's not the same. People care more about people in the Midwest."

O'Brien's real estate career, which began in Madison in 1974, has thrived there. O'Brien opened her own firm, brokering both commercial and residential properties, shortly after earning her real estate license. "I never sold a piece of real estate before I started my own company," she says. But she went into business for herself because "I wanted to grow as much as I could grow without someone say-

Based in a 6,200-square-foot brick building on the West Beltline, Mardi O'Brien Real Estate, Inc., provides services for residential and commercial sales and property management.

ing 'stop'."

O'Brien is convinced that a solid grounding in the principles of real estate is the key to her success; her first year in business she spent 63 days in school. "If you're going to be the best in any field, you need to be the most knowledgeable," she says. Among the many professional real estate designations that she has earned are Certified Commercial Investment Member (CCIM), which involved 4.5 years of study, and Certified Real Estate Broker Manager (CRB). O'Brien continues to study real estate principles in formal coursework and also has taught courses in real estate.

O'Brien is a leader in the real estate field both locally and nationally. She serves on the national CCIM Council and has been a national director for the National Association of Realtors, president of the Madison and the Wisconsin Apartment Owners Associations, as well as a director of the Greater Madison Board of Realtors, the first female president of the board in 1979, and its Realtor of the Year in 1982.

O'Brien's many community activities include service on the board of the Greater Madison Chamber of Commerce; in 1982 she

was its first female chairman. She was also chairman of the Dane County chapter of the American Heart Association. O'Brien was named Woman of the Year by the Madison Business and Professional Women's Club in 1980 and a Woman of Distinction by the Greater Madison YWCA in 1985.

Mardi O'Brien Real Estate, Inc., is based in a 6,200-square-foot brick building on the West Beltline, and its services include residential and commercial sales and property management. In the future O'Brien hopes to become involved in commercial or residential development.

Hooper Construction Corporation

Founded in 1913 as a heating contractor, Hooper Construction Corporation has grown to include three divisions— Mechanical, Electrical, and Electric Power—and is headquartered at 2030 Pennsylvania Avenue in Madison.

In an era when swings in the economy determine whether we are in the midst of rebuilding or expansion, it is necessary to be able to thrive in either situation. "Obviously, it is more difficult to reconstruct a sewage treatment plant or a power line while it's being used than it is to build a new one," says Donald N. Gardner, president of Hooper Construction Corporation. Continuous and heavy use of existing facilities creates a need for highly skilled service. Greater expertise is needed to combine today's new technology with older facilities.

When it comes to building expansion, Hooper Construction offers invaluable field experience combined with design, engineering, and construction services necessary to meet the requirements of increased growth.

In addition to working with the most up-to-date technology in

a wide variety of mechanical, electrical, and electric power projects, Hooper often faces the challenges of inclement weather and less-than-ideal ground conditions. An example is a project that involved installing a fiber-optic cable from Chicago to Minneapolis. Despite near record-breaking rains, Hooper met its deadlines, enabling the other contractors and subcontractors to complete their portions of the project on time.

Another weather-related challenge was stringing new power lines across the Dane County Mud Lake/Goose Lake public preserve area in a large peat bog that local residents call the "bottomless swamp."

Hooper, serving as the job's general contractor, designed and created a series of "frozen roads" that could be used as "ice barges" for transporting the steel utility poles into the swamp. According to the client, Hooper's performance on the job was "highly commendable."

Hooper Construction, founded in 1913 by Charles A. Hooper as a heating contractor, is today a contracting firm with three major divisions: Mechanical, Electrical, and Electric Power. Hooper works on both new construction and renovations and always emphasizes high quality. "It's unusual for a contracting firm to have professional engineers involved in project management," Gardner says. Hooper's blend of field people and professionals such as engineers helps give the firm an edge in project management, which is crucial to the

Manchester Place, a 10-story building located directly across the square from the State Capitol, is an example of the new life being infused into the downtown area. Hooper Construction Corporation was the electrical and plumbing contractor on the project.

success of most construction projects. This diversification of services enables Hooper to offer turnkey construction, making it a one-stop organization for many projects.

Hooper has long utilized a design/build approach, which teams the contractors with the architect at the beginning of the design process to allow for increased flexibility and more efficiency, resulting in a lower cost to the client.

Manchester Place on the Capitol Square, a new Madison landmark, is a recent example of Hooper's design/build approach. Hooper was the subcontractor for the electrical and plumbing work for the 10-story, 120,000-square-foot office building complete with six-level parking ramp. For this project Hooper made full use of its in-house computer-aided drafting (CAD) system, which reduces drafting time up to 50 percent, as well as its custom-designed job-cost system, which reevaluates the costs on a building if construction is ahead or behind schedule or if there are variances in labor.

A mainstay of Hooper Construction's business is power lines. Clients consist of major investor-owned electric utilities, RECs, and municipal utilities in a five-state area that rely on the company's Electric Power Division for everything from transmission, distribution, underground, substations, founda-

Madison Metropolitan Sewage District's Nine Springs Wastewater Treatment Plant has undergone seven additions to its basic facility. Hooper Construction Corporation's Mechanical Division has been a part of five of these projects.

tions, and the tree-trimming services necessary to keep electric power lines clear of interference. "It's not very glamorous," says Gardner, "but power lines are essential to every aspect of business."

Hooper's Electrical Division has been in existence for more than 40 years. Projects have included electrical design and installation in structures such as large warehouses and office buildings, as well as lighting systems for parking ramps and installation of electronic sensors in airport runways. The Electrical Division's capabilities include industrial and commercial wiring, design and engineering, and protective lighting.

Hooper's Mechanical Division has done work in hydroelectric, fossil-fuel, and nuclear power plants throughout Wisconsin. Hooper has also provided services for numerous sewage and waste-

water treatment plants. The Mechanical Division's capabilities include power plant and process piping, certified pipe welding, HVAC, industrial refrigeration, plumbing and drainage, pollution control, water and wastewater treatment plants, energy management, industrial and commercial sheet-metal work, and stainless-steel fabrication. Hooper's computerized plasma cutting machine, one of the first in use by a contracting firm in Wisconsin, significantly reduces the time involved in making complex sheet-metal fittings.

Hooper Construction Corporation is a privately held company whose shareholders are all active employees. "We encourage ownership to manifest growth and perpetuate the company," Gardner explains. The firm has a payroll of $10 million per year and employs an average of 300 people. The company, which is based on Madison's East Side on an 11-acre site near Tenney Park, has completed more than 4,700 projects in its 75 years of existence and has seen a growth in annual revenues from $15 million to $25 million in the past five years.

This 138-kilovolt transmission line running from Rockdale to Fitchburg, near Madison, is representative of the many power lines and substations Hooper Construction Corporation has built and maintained for the electric utilities in a five-state area since 1948.

CHAPTER ELEVEN

Quality of Life

M edical and educational
institutions contribute to
the quality of life of
Madison-area residents.

Photo by Karl R. Lechten

Dean Medical Center

When Dr. Joseph Dean opened his small office at the corner of State and Mifflin streets in Madison in 1904, little did he know the impact that his name and practice would have on the future health care needs of southern Wisconsin residents. Now, as the twentieth century comes to a close, Dean Medical Center has become one of the largest multispecialty clinics in the United States. With 15 clinic locations and two Urgent Care centers in Dane County, Dean recorded a half-million patient visits to more than 200 physicians in 1988.

While growth has been an important part in the history of Dean, its mission has not changed in almost 90 years. Dean Medical Center and its 1,000 employees are committed to providing the highest quality in health care. Caring for patients is the most important ingredient in Dean's success.

Keys to delivering excellence of care include up-to-date knowledge and equipment; state-of-the-art facilities; competent, well-trained support staff; and, most important, a skilled medical staff. Dean offers a number of pioneering surgical and noninvasive medical services to southern Wisconsin. Utilization of laser and other technology by Dean physicians has resulted in increased outpatient procedures that in the past involved costly and often lengthy hospitalization. In addition to specialists and subspecialists, Dean Medical Center offers a full range of primary care for rou-

Using up-to-date knowledge and equipment; state-of-the-art facilities; a competent, well-trained support staff; and a skilled medical staff, Dean Medical Center offers many pioneering surgical and noninvasive medical services to southern Wisconsin.

Dean Medical Center and its 1,000 employees are committed to providing the highest-quality health care.

tine physical examinations and health maintenance for the entire family.

In 1983 the insurance arm of Dean Medical Center was formed. DeanCareHMO is now the third-largest health maintenance organization in Wisconsin with 100,000 enrollees and more than 600 health care providers. Like traditional health insurance, HMOs provide coverage for medical care when a patient is sick or injured, but unlike most insurance plans, DeanCare-HMO also provides coverage to help the patient and his family stay well.

The Dean Foundation for Health, Research, and Education was founded in 1986. The foundation is a nonprofit, public service organization that conducts medical research, and provides educational opportunities for professionals and researchers in health-related fields, as well as the general public.

In order to assure the highest-possible standards for quality health care, the Dean Medical Center is accredited by the Accreditation Association of Ambulatory Health Care (AAAHC).

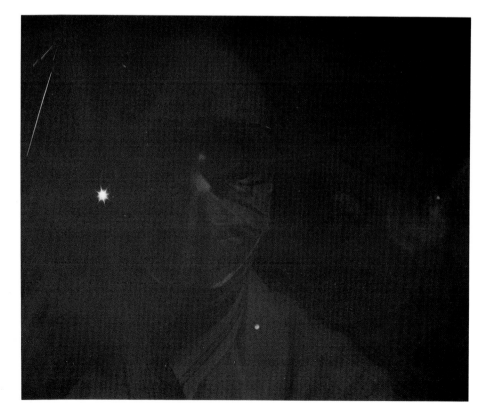

Meriter Hospital

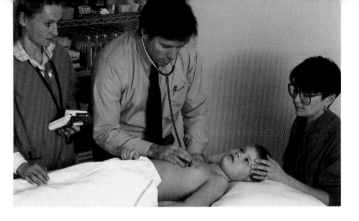

"With 2,250 employees, Meriter Hospital is one of the largest private employers in Dane County," according to Terri Potter, president of Meriter Hospital. "We serve about 31,000 people in our emergency room each year, and we have 84,000 other outpatient visits and 115,000 inpatient days per year. We have 345 physicians on our active and associate medical staff, 135 clergy members from more than 15 denominations, and 650 dedicated volunteers."

Despite its size, Meriter Hospital still puts service to patients first. "We are concentrating on high quality day-to-day patient ser-

Meriter Hospital's Birthing Center is the first to offer single-room maternity care to Madison-area mothers-to-be. Each of the suites is designed to make sure each family's birthing experience is an intimate, special event.

vices and innovative options for health-care delivery. We want to be recognized for our service to patients," Potter says.

Meriter has developed many new programs in response to changes in the health-care delivery field. Meriter Hospital's Same Day Surgery, Women's Center, Physical Medicine and Rehabilitation, Adoles-

cent Psychiatry, NewStart ("the caring alcoholism/drug treatment program"), Cardiac Rehabilitation, and Center for Health Promotion programs all incorporate Meriter's commitment to "emphasizing personalized care in the delivery of services." That commitment extends to new residents of the community through the Doctor For You free physician referral service that provides access to more than 270 doctors.

Innovation in health-care delivery also applies to Meriter Hospital's sister corporations. Meriter Enterprises has developed a Home Health Division that offers mobile X-ray and pharmacy services, and Meriter Retirement Services offers an Adult Day Care Center program for older adults.

Meriter Hospital has two campuses, one located on Park Street and the other near the capitol building in downtown Madison. The institution—formed in 1987 from the merger of the two oldest hospitals in Madison, Methodist and Madison General—is part of Meriter Health Services, Inc.

Meriter Health Services, a not-for-profit corporation, sets policies and oversees operations for Meriter Hospital (with its two campuses); Meriter Retirement Services (which includes Methodist Retirement Center, Elderhouse, and Methodist Health Center); Meriter Foundation; Madison General Hospital Medical and Surgical Foundation; and Meriter Health Enterprises (which includes its General Medical Laboratories and Meriter Home Health

Emergency services is an important part of the comprehensive health care package offered at Meriter. The hospital's emergency rooms serve more than 31,000 people annually.

Divisions).

The name Meriter is derived from the root word merit, which emphasizes Meriter's commitment to quality and excellence. "We provide quality services and personal care to our patients, residents, and customers," Potter says.

That commitment to patient care is enhanced through Meriter's relationship with a number of major medical groups, including Physicians Plus (a consortium of 26 formerly independent physician groups), Associated Physicians, Bone and Joint Surgery Associates, and psychiatric providers. Meriter Hospital is also a major teaching affiliate of the UW-Madison Medical School, offering resident physicians training in many specialties.

The largest service at Meriter Hospital is surgery. More than 20,000 surgical procedures are performed annually in Meriter's operating rooms, on both an inpatient and outpatient basis. These surgeries include general surgery, as well as gynecological; plastics; dental; ophthalmological; orthopedic; ear, nose, and throat; neurosurgical; thoracic; cardiovascular; and urological. Two outpatient

surgery sites—one at each campus—serve as self-contained outpatient surgical facilities with several treatment and operating rooms, as well as a recovery area designed to provide comfort and stimulate a rapid recovery from the effects of surgery.

Medical services are Meriter Hospital's second-largest service. Medical specialties and subspecialties include gastroenterology, oncology, neurology, eating disorders, endocrinology, nephrology, and psychiatry.

Meriter Hospital has a long history of offering many medical firsts to the Madison area. The hospital had the first intensive-care units in Madison, and critically ill medical and surgical patients continue to receive highly skilled nursing care and medical supervision in the hos-

Cardiac rehabilitation is one of many programs offered at Meriter's Center for Health Promotion, an impressive facility that houses a running track and the latest in physical fitness equipment. The Center for Health Promotion programs are open to employees and the public.

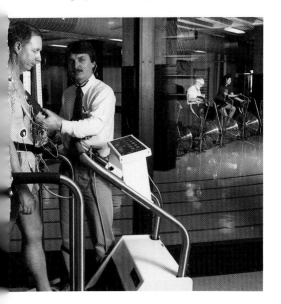

pital's Intensive Care and Special Care units.

Meriter also offers one of the most comprehensive heart-care programs in Wisconsin. A highly skilled and dedicated team of heart professionals works closely to oversee a patient's care from diagnosis through treatment or surgery and into the rehabilitation phase, where necessary. Meriter's cardiac-care program includes high-risk factor detection and prevention services, noninvasive diagnostic testing, cardiac catheterization and angioplasty (including laser technology), open-heart surgery, implantation of pacemakers, cardiac rehabilitation, and education.

The hospital provided another first—this time in the area of obstetrics—with its Birthing Center. The Birthing Center features Single-Room Maternity Care, complete with a mother/baby nursing model. That means Meriter is the first, and only, hospital in the Madison area that can offer mothers and infants the same private suite during their entire stay, from admittance to discharge. And Meriter, in partnership with UW-Madison, houses a nationally recognized regional center for high-risk obstetrical and neonatal care.

Meriter Hospital has adopted a mission statement that exemplifies its commitment to the people it serves, an approach that emphasizes the community at large and its needs. In addition to providing

quality health care services, Meriter's commitment in this area is apparent through the many educational programs and conferences it offers.

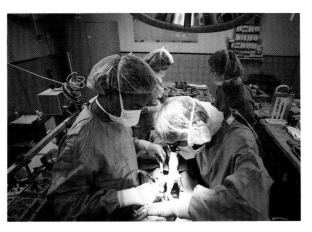

Meriter's Cardiology/Cardiovascular Surgery Department has been a leader in offering advanced subspecialty diagnosis and treatment. Meriter was the first community hospital in Madison to perform open-heart surgery.

Potter emphasizes that commitment. "Meriter is the only Madison hospital that is locally owned and operated, and does not have to respond to government oversight," he says. "We're just here for the Madison and southern Wisconsin communities."

That commitment to excellence also envelops all Meriter employees. "We think it is important to emphasize the family and problems families deal with," Potter says. "With 60 percent of preschool moms working, we think child-care issues are very important." Meriter Hospital offers a child-care center for the hospital's working parents, and Ginger Ail™, a day-care service for sick children of any parent in the community.

St. Marys Hospital Medical Center

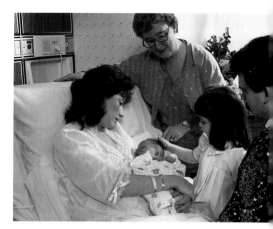

"We came at the invitation of the community, and we continue to be an active part of the community," says Gerald Lefert, president of St. Marys Hospital Medical Center and its first lay administrator.

For nearly 80 years St. Marys Hospital Medical Center has served Madison on the two-acre site near Lake Wingra that was given to the Sisters of St. Mary for the Sisters' first hospital in Wisconsin. As Madison has grown up around it, the hospital with a heart has found itself located in the heart of the city—without ever moving.

The founding Sisters of St. Mary, based in St. Louis, Missouri, are today known as the Franciscan Sisters of Mary. Their SSM Health Care System owns a number of health care facilities in several states.

More babies have been born at St. Marys than at any other area hospital. With a complete range of birthing options and services, St. Marys has long recognized the need for the total family to share in the birth process. Photo by Bob Rashid

When St. Marys opened in 1912, it was staffed by eight Sisters, four doctors, and four nurses. The staff today includes more than 1,600 hospital staff members and more than 500 medical staff members. St. Marys' buildings have changed, too, but the hospital's mission has remained the same. "Building additions, changes in the size and scope of the hospital, and advancements in technology have been made while the spirit of those early Sisters has been maintained: providing expert health

facility houses two outpatient services, a surgery center for procedures not requiring hospitalization, and six pediatric clinics. The clinics include a follow-up clinic for infants who have been in intensive care, the neurodevelopmental clinic, the hydrocephalus and spinal deformity clinic, the respiratory disease clinic, the pediatric cardiology clinic, and the attention deficit disorder clinic. Facilities located elsewhere on the West Side include St. Marys Adult Day Health Center and St. Marys Health Works, a community health education center.

St. Marys is a statewide leader in the care of babies and in cardiac services. Today more babies have been born at St. Marys than at any other area hospital. Its Infant Intensive Care Unit is staffed around the clock with neonatologists trained in the care of sick infants. St. Marys is also Madison's busiest heart hospital. It was a leader in using techniques such as balloon angioplasty, in which clogged arteries can be opened by inflating a tiny balloon inside them.

All this experience makes a significant difference in the quality of care at St. Marys Hospital Medical Center, Lefert believes. "Experience counts," he says. "It's common knowledge in medical circles that the best care is given where the staff is the most experienced."

St. Marys, the hospital with a heart, is located near Lake Wingra at 707 South Mills Street. Since it opened in 1912 the hospital's mission has remained the same as the founding Sisters of St. Mary— personalized care and service to the sick, recognizing the totality of each person, and the intimate interrelatedness of body and spirit. Its tradition has been one of providing the very best care and the very latest in medical technology.

care, mindful of the physical, spiritual, and emotional needs of each patient," according to Lefert.

Most of St. Marys' services are provided at its main facility at 707 South Mills Street on Madison's Near West Side, where it is licensed for 440 hospital beds. Just behind the hospital is the Dean/St. Marys Surgery and Care Center at 800 South Brooks Street. This

Edgewood College

Edgewood College is "the small campus with big advantages," according to James A. Ebben, president since 1987. "As a Catholic college, Edgewood places a high priority on the liberal arts, personal development, and service to the community," Ebben relates. "And at a time when the need for strengthening the fabric of American society has never been greater, Edgewood is responding with a moral and ethical education. All this is part of the Sinsinawa Dominican tradition, an Edgewood hallmark since it was founded in 1927."

As its name implies, Edgewood's 55-acre wooded campus is located on the edge of a much larger wooded area—Vilas Park, Lake Wingra, and the University of Wisconsin Arboretum. Students can swim, sail, or fish in Lake Wingra (and ice skate in the winter); visit the Vilas Park Zoo; or cross-country ski, hike, or bicycle in the 1,200-acre arboretum. And during class time, the Mazzuchelli Field Station on Lake Wingra has a natural freshwater lab right outside to complement the biology, anatomy, physiology, and microbiology laboratories inside.

Students who do not want to attend a large, impersonal institution choose Edgewood for its personalized approach to education. With a student-faculty ratio of 12 to one and classes that seldom exceed 16

The sun rises over Lake Wingra and Mazzuchelli Field Station (seen in background, lower left).

De Ricci Hall houses administrative offices and classrooms.

students, Edgewood allows all students an opportunity to get to know faculty members personally. All full-time faculty members serve as academic advisers as well as teachers. "Because professors know individual students' personal strengths as well as their academic performance, they can provide potential employers or graduate schools with insightful recommendations," Ebben says.

Roughly 1,250 students currently attend Edgewood. Of those, 475 are full-time undergraduates (160 of whom live on campus in two residence halls). The rest of the

students are enrolled in the Weekend Degree and Graduate programs, which are designed to serve the community by offering opportunities for working adults to earn college degrees.

A comprehensive liberal arts institution, Edgewood offers major and minor programs in more than 20 disciplines. Edgewood offers majors in all areas of the arts and sciences, as well as programs in business, medical technology, special education, criminal justice, public policy, nursing, computer information systems, child life, and other specialties. The faculty is made up of some 85 full- and part-time professors.

Approximately 25 Sinsinawa Sisters are affiliated with the campus, although not all of them are teaching faculty. The congregation of the Sinsinawa Dominican Sisters was founded in 1848 in Sinsinawa, Wisconsin. Former state governor Cadwallader C. Washburn presented Edgewood's campus to the Sinsinawa Sisters in 1881 to be "used for educational purposes of the highest order."

University of Wisconsin Hospital and Clinics

"In contrast to many cities this size, Madison is very fortunate to have a major medical center such as the University of Wisconsin Hospital and Clinics," says Gordon Derzon, superintendent of the hospital since 1975. "We are proud of the comprehensive, high-quality services we offer the public. Our capabilities are very sophisticated, yet we also provide high-quality, accessible routine medical care." The medical center sponsors U-CARE HMO, a health maintenance organization.

Today UW Hospital and Clinics is "a major teaching institution and a leading center for patient care, biomedical research, education of health professionals, and public service," according to Linda Sunshine and John W. Wright, who included it as one of the nation's 64 outstanding health care facilities in their book *The Best Hospitals in America.*

In addition to inpatient facilities, UW Hospital and Clinics maintains more than 80 outpatient clinics. The 24-hour-per-day UW MedFlight helicopter is an airborne critical care service that provides immediate and skilled emergency care during the rapid transport of critically ill or injured patients

Today the University of Wisconsin Hospital and Clinics is at the forefront of health care delivery, offering comprehensive, high-quality services.

within a 225-mile radius of Madison. In addition, the UW Children's Hospital inpatient, outpatient, and home care services meet the needs of infants, children, and adolescents.

UW Hospital and Clinics is well known for a wide variety of innovative and high-quality health care services. One of the best known is the UW Clinical Cancer Center (UWCCC), a comprehensive center funded by the National Cancer Institute that has become a national leader in cancer research, education, and treatment, particularly for breast and urologic cancers. UWCCC researchers were among the first to demonstrate that the drug tamoxifen could prevent the recurrence of breast cancer in certain women and to investigate the anti-cancer effect of interleukin-2 and interferon. Nearly 15,000 outpatient visits are recorded in the medical oncology clinic annually, while the radiation clinic registers 30,000 visits. Another 1,300 people are admitted each year for cancer care.

Another major service is the organ transplantation program, one of the largest and most successful in the nation. The efforts of the UW transplant team, coupled with excellent cooperation from hospitals throughout the state, have earned Wisconsin the highest per capita rate of organ donation in

Described as a "major teaching institution and a leading center for patient care, biomedical research, education of health professionals, and public service," the University of Wisconsin Hospital and Clinics is ranked as one of the nation's 64 outstanding health care facilities in *The Best Hospitals in America.*

the country. UW Hospital and Clinics' kidney, liver, pancreas, heart, lung, cornea, and bone-marrow transplantation programs are widely respected.

Beyond its patient care, teaching, research, and community service missions, UW Hospital and Clinics also has a considerable economic impact (estimated to be more than $500 million per year) within the state. In addition, UW Hospital and Clinics, with 3,800 employees, is one of Madison's largest employers.

UW Hospital and Clinics has been a major health care resource in Wisconsin since its founding as Wisconsin General Hospital in 1924. Says Derzon, "Our intention is to continue to be in the forefront of health care delivery, which is consistent with our academic, research, and community service missions."

The Marketplace

M adison's retail establishments, service industries,
and products are enjoyed
by residents and visitors.

Photo by Bruce Fritz

Ahrens Cadillac-Oldsmobile

In 1964, when Peter Ahrens moved his car dealership to Applegate Road, just off what is now the West Beltline, his six acres of land were in the country. Fish Hatchery Road was two lanes wide, and the Ahrens dealership was surrounded by farmland. "We had cows watching our service area at first," Ahrens says. "I was the first car dealer to move out here."

Once his competitors saw how well he did selling cars among the cows, however, they began to follow him out. "I tripled my business the first year I moved out here," he explains. Today Ahrens Cadillac-Oldsmobile, a privately held corporation, is the largest retailer of Oldsmobiles in Wisconsin.

Ahrens opened his dealership in 1962 in downtown Madison. He had worked for Motors Holding, a division of General Motors, for nine years before he decided to open a dealership himself. "Motors Holding financed the land and the building," the entrepreneur says. "I paid them off in three years."

Ahrens learned a lot about car dealerships in his nine years at Motors Holding. "I got one million dollars' worth of experience running dealerships for GM," he says. Motors Holding financed 75 percent of a dealership and kept a watchful eye on its investments. "I opened a lot of dealerships and

Peter Ahrens, owner/founder of Ahrens Cadillac-Oldsmobile, in his office on Applegate Road.

closed a lot of dealerships," Ahrens notes. "I worked with all kinds of dealerships in different areas. I talked to dealers who said their businesses weren't doing well because their city's economy was depressed. And yet other dealers with the same product in the same city were doing well. It wasn't the location; it was the dealer's business methods that made the difference."

Ahrens, who earned a B.A. at Notre Dame and an M.B.A. at Harvard, says that he learned to watch inventory very closely when he worked at Motors Holding. "I learned what things were worth—leases, buildings, used cars—

because I had to auction them off."

He also credits his father for his success in the automobile business. "My father was an extremely successful salesman. He taught me a lot."

Ahrens and his wife, Margo, have seven children. Don J. Ahrens, one of their sons, is now assistant sales manager; Peter, Don, and Margo (along with Dick Stroud) are on the board of directors of Ahrens Cadillac-Oldsmobile.

Business continues to be good on Applegate Road. "If we had more inventory of Cadillacs, we could sell more," Ahrens says. "That's kind of a nice problem."

Concourse Hotel and Governor's Club

"Our location is second to none in the state of Wisconsin," says Darrell R. Wild, managing general partner of the Concourse Hotel and Governor's Club. "They aren't going to build or create another capitol." The value of being near the capitol is "more than just the building," according to Wild, although close-up views of the capitol and nearby lakes are available through many of the Concourse's windows. "It's the power of all the officeholders and all the decision-makers" located in the capitol and nearby buildings. Wild points out that Wisconsin's state government is "a huge industry; many people who stay at the Concourse are in town to meet with government leaders."

Wild values the Concourse's downtown location for more than just its proximity to the capitol. "Suburbs all look alike," he says. "A suburb could be anywhere. The only thing that's unique about a city is its downtown. There's only one Times Square, one Michigan Avenue—and one State Street." He points out that the enormous purchasing power of UW-Madison's nearly 44,000 students supports State Street's unique and ever-changing stores.

Wild believes that the Concourse's location makes it an ideal base for people who want to sightsee. "Most people who stay at the Concourse fly in," he says. "They take the shuttle from the airport, and then they can walk up and down State Street—possibly the most unique street in the state." Wild often suggests to hotel guests that they take a walk down State Street, but sometimes finds it a challenge to try to explain what it's like if they've never seen it. "I know some type of entertainment will be going on—a sax player, an oboist, a violinist or guitarist, maybe someone playing the harmonica. I don't know what it will be, but there will be something," he states.

Wild, one of the limited partners who built the Concourse in 1974, reports that no one ever comes back disappointed with State Street. "I've never sent a guest down to State Street who didn't come back with a story," he says.

The largest hotel in Madison, the Concourse has a total of 376 guest rooms, including 103 rooms in the Governor's Club. Free parking for registered guests is available in a 265-car underground parking ramp. First on Dayton is a casual yet elegant restaurant serving breakfast, lunch, and an extensive dinner menu featuring American and Continental cuisine, as well as an award-winning Sunday champagne brunch. There is entertainment nightly in the piano bar lounge.

The Concourse Hotel and Governor's Club offers guests complimentary use of a fitness center with exercise equipment, massage therapist, heated pool, outdoor hot tub, sauna, steam bath, and tanning bed. A full-service hair salon, valet service, limousine rental, office services, and gift shop are also located in the hotel. Room service is available from 6:30 a.m. until midnight.

The largest hotel in Madison with a total of 376 guest rooms and 103 rooms in the Governor's Club, the Concourse Hotel and Governor's Club has a prime location downtown near the capitol.

The Concourse is Madison's largest convention hotel, offering a full variety of meeting rooms and setups in 22,500 square feet of meeting and exhibit space. The hotel's staff of 260 includes an experienced catering staff and group-meeting services staff.

A unique feature of the Concourse is its three-story Governor's Club, "a luxurious hotel within the hotel, designed with the discriminating traveler in mind," according to Wild. The Governor's Club offers travelers concierge service, a private keyed elevator, Continental breakfast and weekday paper, king rooms and suites with upgraded furnishings and travel amenities, desk, bedside and bathroom telephones, complimentary in-room sodas and juice, turndown service with cookies, a private lounge overlooking the capitol, express check-in and check-out services, and a midnight snack for late arrivals.

Complimentary evening cocktails and hors d'oeuvres and Continental breakfast are available in the private Governor's Club Lounge, which overlooks the capitol through a wall of glass. The Governor's Club Lounge, open only to Governor's Club residents, is hung with large portraits of the governors of Wisconsin. It has a working fire-

place, comfortable sofas and chairs, and a bar.

All rooms in the Governor's Club offer king-size beds, elegant furnishings, remote cable television, multiple telephones, hair dryers, and signature bathrobes. Every room has a view of either the capitol building or Lake Mendota. The Governor's Club rooms include executive rooms and several varieties of suites. The Governor's Suites include parlor rooms with a dining/conference table, a chandelier, sofas and chairs, a kitchen area with wet bar and microwave, an entertainment unit with television and VCR, two telephones, and a powder room. Jacuzzi Suites feature a king-size canopy bed, leisure area, and Ja-

The three-story Governor's Club is a luxurious hotel located within the hotel designed with the discriminating traveler in mind. One of the many amenities is a private lounge overlooking the capitol where evening cocktails and hors d'oeuvres and Continental breakfasts are served.

cuzzi surrounded by beveled mirrors and lights. Senator's Suites offer parlor areas with wet bar and refrigerator, as well as entertainment units, conference table, and two telephones.

Says Wild, "The Concourse Hotel and Governor's Club is a full-service hotel and a luxury hotel combined to offer the best service, location, and value."

Gordon Flesch Company, Inc.

"I didn't even know what a copy machine was when I started out. I'd never even seen one," says Gordon Flesch, who founded his office equipment company in Madison in 1956. Flesch had been selling Royal Typewriters and was approached by 3M to open a copy machine dealership. "Three weeks later I was a dealer," he says. "I didn't have any customers at first, and I did everything myself. I sold the machines, I shipped them, and I serviced them." Luckily, at first very few of the machines he sold needed servicing. "I knew how to change a belt and a lamp. That's basically all I knew how to do until I hired a serviceman."

Today the Gordon Flesch Company, Inc., employs more than 300 factory-trained service personnel as well as an entire department of customer-support representatives. The privately held corporation is

The firm sells several lines of copy equipment as well as information-processing and facsimile products.

still a family-owned operation with a friendly approach to business. "People can call any officer in this company—any officer," he says.

A lot of credit for the success of his business goes to his early association with 3M. "There were only 65 3M dealers in the United States at the time, so we got an outstanding education on how to run a business," says Gordon Flesch. "We were good dealers because of them—they taught us how to do things the right way.

"Today the Gordon Flesch Company is probably the largest privately held office equipment company in the United States." According to Gordon Flesch, "What differentiates us from other office equipment companies is creative selling. Not a lot of people walk in the door and ask to buy a copier."

Today the firm sells several lines of copy equipment, as well as information-processing and facsimile products. In 1978 the company had 86 employees and sales of $3 million. Today it employs 500 people and has sales of $44 million. "The future looks great. We should double our size in five years."

John Flesch, Gordon's son, who is also active in the firm, anticipates continued growth in sales. "According to Data Resources Inc., an economic forecast group, the office automation industry will exceed the automobile industry in

The Flesch family is active in the company with (clockwise from front) Gordon Flesch, chairman of the board and chief executive officer; Thomas Flesch, president; John Flesch, executive vice-president and treasurer; and William Flesch, vice-president.

total sales by 1992." He points to the recent explosive growth in sales of relatively new products such as facsimile machines and color copiers. "In 1984 we didn't sell FAX machines; however, by 1989 they were 30 percent of our total sales. The FAX machine market just exploded."

New products are crucial to the success of an office equipment company. "Our growth has come because of our product lines," John Flesch says. "We're on the cutting edge of office equipment technology."

His father agrees, "Our business is really product driven. It used to be that a new model of copier would be introduced every year and a half. Now we're getting new models every six months. And it

Today the Gordon Flesch Company has sales of $44 million and employs 500 people.

will be a whole different market-place with color copiers. That's another venture into something that didn't exist two years ago. It's a great time to be in the business."

A second component of the firm's success is its employee base. "Our people are real professionals at their jobs," states Gordon. "I'm really proud of them. A solid core of long-term employees really helps make a company—it gives it a lot of credibility and stability. And our employees have grown along with the company. That's the best part." John points out that "this is typically not a business where employees stay a long time. And yet there are a large number of people who've worked here for 20 years and more."

Gordon agrees: "We keep our people longer than anybody." As part of the draw, he points to the firm's strong employee benefits pro-gram, including profit sharing, em-ployee assistance, 401K plans, and a stock-bonus program.

A third element contributing to

the success of the company is the community where it is based. (There are now branch offices in West Allis, Wisconsin; Columbus, Ohio; and St. Charles and Lom-bard, Illinois.) "Madison is just so much a part of this company," John Flesch says.

"There isn't any boom or bust in Madison," Gordon points out. "The stability comes because Madi-son is a small market dominated by the state and university." In addi-tion to the stable economy, Gordon cites excellent schools and clean gov-ernment as advantages of the local economy. "Our schools have to be about as good as they get, and our govern-ment is clean as a whis-tle at all levels."

There are four members of the Flesch family active in the com-pany today. Gordon Flesch is chairman of the board and chief exec-utive officer; Thomas (in Columbus, Ohio), is pres-ident; John (in Madison, Wisconsin), is executive vice-president and trea-surer; and William (in St. Charles, Illinois), is a

vice-president. "I'm really blessed," Gordon Flesch says. "It's been a great 34 years. It's nice to have young sons. It's great for the em-ployees. They know the company's going to be here for a long time. And my sons really work at it—they don't take it for granted."

Gordon and his wife, Rozanne, have strong ties to the Madison com-munity. They both graduated from UW-Madison, and their five chil-dren (including two daughters, Lucy Heironimus and Sally Cox, who are not active in the com-pany) attended various UW system schools. Over the years the Gor-don Flesch Company, Inc., has been active in the community. Its in-volvement has included support of the UW-Madison athletic depart-ment, the McClain Center, Channel 21, and the United Way of Dane County.

One of the many distinguishing factors that makes the Gordon Flesch Company better than the competition is its creative ap-proach to sales.

East Towne Suites

"The suite concept is more than just a bed in a room," says Loraine Zeier, co-owner, with her husband, Raymond Zeier, of East Towne Suites, located near the intersection of I90-94 and U.S. 151 (East Washington Avenue). The all-suites hotel, which opened in November 1987, appeals to a different market than a more traditional hotel, according to the Zeiers. "It's more homey than a lot of motels," she adds. "It's so much like home that we've got people coming down to the lobby in their robes, just like they're at home. They feel so relaxed."

Part of the attraction of the lobby is the breakfast nook, where complimentary breakfasts and snacks are served at various times throughout the day; complimentary coffee is always available. Across from the breakfast cafe is an indoor heated pool and an outsize whirlpool.

Complimentary breakfasts are available every day. Guests are welcome to eat in the breakfast cafe or take a tray back to their suites. Complimentary hot soup, cheese, crackers, bottled waters, and fruit juices are served in the late after-

noons. "Our hospitality times offer guests the opportunity to invite associates to join them as guests, with all the comforts of home," according to the Zeiers.

All 123 suites in the hotel offer large, comfortable beds (king, queen, or double size) with studio settings that can provide additional sleeping accommodations. The suites include large six-drawer dressers and upscale construction details such as marble around the tubs instead of tile. All suites have refrigerators, and some have microwaves and wet bars as well. The door to each suite is locked with a state-of-the-art security card lock system.

Each suite has a remote-control television set placed 30 inches high. "That way," says Raymond Zeier, "you can see the TV instead of your feet." Each suite is custom furnished, with its own color scheme, pictures, and other decorative touches.

Despite its many comforts and services, East Towne Suites is relatively low priced. "We aim for the in-between market—between economy and full service," the Zeiers say. Although there is not a restaurant in the hotel, catering can be arranged for meetings or conferences. And microwave ovens, vending machines, and ice machines throughout the hotel allow guests to prepare their own meals and snacks.

Several of the suites are larger "super suites," featuring beds that fold into the wall and extra-large conference tables. Three of the suites feature king-size whirlpool tubs; there is also a Jacuzzi suite. "That's our most popular suite," the Zeiers say. "We should have put more in."

East Towne Suites appeals particularly to business travelers, so each suite features large conference/work tables and computer jacks.

FROM LEFT TO RIGHT:

The East Towne Suites lobby.

The indoor heated pool and outsize whirlpool are just two of the many amenities offered to guests at East Towne Suites.

At the breakfast cafe guests receive complimentary breakfasts every day and complimentary snacks at various times throughout the day.

East Towne Suites is located near the intersection of I90-94 and U.S. 151 (East Washington Avenue).

Other amenities for the business traveler include four large meeting rooms that hold up to 75 people, as well as a boardroom for smaller executive conferences.

East Towne Suites is also an attractive destination for shoppers, since East Towne Mall, with its 100 stores, is adjacent to the hotel. "East Towne Mall is a big draw," Zeier says. "People come for weekends and shop." The mall also includes a multiscreen movie theater, East Towne Cinema; East Gate Cinema.

The Zeiers have owned the land on which East Towne Suites is built for many years; they purchased the former Seventy-Six Farm from Raymond Zeier's father, Leo, beginning in 1964. The original farm was named for the 76-mile-drive to Milwaukee, where the origi-

nal farmers used to take their grain to the brewery. Parts of the original farmland have been preserved as part of a greenway that includes a natural springs called East Springs, where the Zeiers sometimes see watercress growing and watch deer cross the railroad tracks.

The Zeier family has been part of Madison for many years. In 1852 Raymond's great-grandfather, Johnn Zeier, arrived from Bavaria and established a small farm where Truax Field now stands. Part of the farm was shady, and he grew ginseng crops, which were then in demand. His son, John Zeier, was a blacksmith who was also an inventor. He made his own camera and darkroom equipment and became a photographer.

The Zeier family has been in

plastic manufacturing for many years in the same area that his great-grandfather came to as a settler. They brought the first production injection-molding machine to Madison in 1949. Zeier Plastics & Mfg., Inc., has been molding millions of plastic products for home and industry.

For many years the Zeiers planned to build a hotel on the site of the old Seventy-Six Farm, but the time never seemed right. "But finally, so many other people were interested in setting up a hotel there that I took some hotel-motel classes and got started," Zeier says. East Towne Suites was designed by Sieger Architects of Madison and built by Kramer Bros. of Plain. "We had so many people inquiring about our land through the years, and we felt running a hotel would be interesting—and it is interesting."

Selected Bibliography

I. BOOKS

Alexander, John. *An Economic Base Study of Madison, Wisconsin.* Madison: University of Wisconsin School of Commerce, Bureau of Research and Service, 1953.

Durand, Janice. *Getting the Most Out of Madison, A Guide.* Madison: Puzzlebox Press, 1974.

Madison, Dane County and Surrounding Towns: A History and Guide. Madison: William J. Park & Co., 1877.

Madison's Economic Factors. City Plan Commission, 1952.

Madison's Economy, Through Depression and War. City Plan Commission, 1951.

Madison's People. City Plan Commission, 1952.

Mollenhoff, David V. *Madison: A History of the Formative Years.* Dubuque, Ill.: Kendall/Hunt, 1982.

Rath, Sara. *Easy Going: Madison and Dane County.* Madison: Tamarack Press, 1977.

Sunshine, Linda, and John W. Wright. *The Best Hospitals in America.* New York: Holt, 1987.

Thwaites, Reuben Gold. *The Story of Madison, 1836-1900.* Reprint edition. Madison: Roger H. Hart, 1973.

Wisconsin's State Capitol Guide and History. 31st edition.

II. NEWSPAPERS

The Capital Times
Isthmus
The Milwaukee Journal
The Milwaukee Sentinel
The Wisconsin State Journal

III. MAGAZINES

In Business
Madison Magazine
The Wisconsin Business Journal

IV. ADDITIONAL RESOURCES

Dane County Cultural Affairs Commission
Downtown Madison, Inc.
Greater Madison Chamber of Commerce
Greater Madison Convention and Visitor's Bureau
Madison Public Library, Central Branch

Patrons

The following individuals, companies, and organizations have made a valuable commitment to the quality of this publication. Windsor Publications and the Greater Madison Chamber of Commerce gratefully acknowledge their participation in *Greater Madison: Meeting the 21st Century.*

Ahrens Cadillac-Oldsmobile*
Concourse Hotel and Governor's Club*
Dean Medical Center*
DRG Medical Packaging*
East Towne Suites*
Edgewood College*
J.H. Findorff & Son Inc.*
First Realty Group, Inc.
First Wisconsin National Bank of Madison*
Gordon Flesch Company, Inc.*
Graber Industries, Inc.*
Hooper Construction Corporation*
Lathrop & Clark*
Mead & Hunt, Consulting Engineers*
Meriter Hospital*
Mardi O'Brien Real Estate, Inc.*
Placon*
The W.T. Rogers Company*
Rural Insurance Companies*
St. Marys Hospital Medical Center*
Shockley Communications Corporation*
The Stark Company, Realtors*
Tracor Northern*
University of Wisconsin Hospital and Clinics*
Viking Insurance Company of Wisconsin*
Warzyn Engineering Inc.*
Wisconsin Power and Light Company*
WMSN Television*

*Participants in Part Two, "Madison's Enterprises." The stories of these companies and organizations appear in chapters 7 through 12, beginning on page 92.

Index